Surviving Lockdown

2020 has been the year of the virus, and it will not be a mere footnote in history. This book reflects on the unprecedented changes to our lives and the impact on our behaviour as we lived through social isolation during the global COVID-19 pandemic. From sociable creatures of habit, we were forced into a period of uncertainty, restriction and risk, physically separated from families and friends.

Packed with guidance and coping strategies for lockdown, this book, authored by top psychologist David Cohen, explores the impact of this widespread quarantine on our relationships, our children, our mental health and our daily lives. Benedictine monks, hermit popes, Dorothy Sayers, Daniel Defoe (who made the isolated Robinson Crusoe a hero), Sigmund Freud and a rabbi's angry dog are all among the cast of characters as we are taken on a whistle-stop tour through plagues in history and brain science, to the importance of introspection and how to make meaning from lockdown. In his trademark entertaining style, Cohen examines the psychology behind our behaviour during this unusual time to discover what we can learn about human nature, what lessons we can learn for the future – and whether we will apply them.

David Cohen is a prolific writer, filmmaker and psychologist.

Surviving Lockdown

Human Nature in Social Isolation

David Cohen

Routledge
Taylor & Francis Group

LONDON AND NEW YORK

First published 2021
by Routledge
2 Park Square, Milton Park, Abingdon, Oxon OX14 4RN

and by Routledge
52 Vanderbilt Avenue, New York, NY 10017

Routledge is an imprint of the Taylor & Francis Group, an informa business

British Library Cataloguing-in-Publication Data
A catalogue record for this book is available from the British Library

Library of Congress Cataloging-in-Publication Data
A catalog record for this book has been requested

ISBN: 978-0-367-61301-3 (pbk)
ISBN: 978-1-003-10509-1 (ebk)

Typeset in Garamond
by Apex CoVantage, LLC

Contents

25.2

Acknowledgements

I owe a great deal to my editor Lucy Kennedy who was sharp, always encouraging and very astute. The only other time I have been so well edited was when Peter Mayer (a publishing legend since he saved Penguin) took on my book on how Freud escaped from Vienna in 1938 with the help of a 'good' Nazi. Maria Andrews helped, competent as ever with checking facts and the references.

Preface

I have personal experience of social isolation though I've only spent one day in jail as a prisoner and never been put in solitary confinement in a psychiatric hospital.

In 1962, under pressure from my father, my mother left me to go to Israel to sell a flat they owned. I was 12. Three weeks later he left to live with his long-standing lover, Evi. I had to conceal from my school that I was on my own because I was sure I would be sent to an orphanage if they found out.

I saw my father every Friday night for dinner and he gave me money for food and fares. After we said goodbye I knew I would not see anyone till Monday morning when I went back to school. So I know something about coping with isolation.

Still I dedicate this book to my mother. If I had ever been isolated with her she would have exasperated me. She complained constantly and was unhappy and nervous, but she was also a fitness fanatic; she could do the splits when she was 70. She would have seen isolation as a great opportunity to practice every gymnastic exercise ever conceived. And nag me to exercise too.

So this is dedicated to Dolly Cohen.

Introduction

Since the 1720s the British Prime Minister has lived and worked at 10 Downing Street. As they follow in the footsteps of the greats like Churchill and Attlee, you would imagine anyone who got to No. 10 would date their letters. Boris Johnson, however, didn't bother with dating his only letter to me. Its message was almost military. Coronavirus was a national emergency and the Prime Minister ordered me and 1.8 million others: 'Stay Home Save Lives'. Four snappy words that echoed the four-word World War II mantra 'Careless talk costs lives'.

Only now, 'Careless walks cost lives', for myself and the 1.8 million others who needed 'sheltering', which means we have a serious or potentially serious condition and should only go outside for medical help or in a dire emergency. On 1 June people in my condition were allowed to go out of our flats and houses briefly. But I should put at least two metres between me and anyone else unless they were part of my household. Two metres is actually more than the width of a super king-size bed.

Boris Johnson, whose social views are liberal, then warned:

> These rules must be observed. So if people break the rules, the police will issue fines and disperse gatherings.

I wonder how many police officers are secretly delighted. Like Dixon of Dock Green in the innocent 1950s, they can now dispense on-the-spot justice. A clout round the earhole. A punch on the nose for repeat offenders. For the good of society.

Officers also now have a chance to practise their verbal skills on those loitering and littering the streets: "On your way and don't let me see you outside till we get the all-clear or you'll be fined."

The British have been obedient on the whole. The Chief Constable of Essex noted that in from mid-April to May 2020, his officers warned over 8,000 people for breaking the social distancing and other rules, but only had to fine 17 incorrigibles.

When it comes, and it is far off from when I am writing this in June 2020, the all-clear will not be like the all-clear in the Blitz. The massed bombers of the virus don't head back across the Channel at the end of their raid. Comparisons with the war are inevitable as the restrictions in 1940–1945 are the nearest to those we have now. The war also taught that humour could help alleviate distress. The subject of this book is totally serious but there are deliberate moments of laughter too. The situation is grim, but to make it all totally grim whittles away at morale.

Human beings are, as Edgar Rice Burroughs (1916), the creator of Tarzan, puts it in *The Beasts of Tarzan,*

> creatures of habit, and when the seeming necessity for schooling ourselves in new ways ceases to exist, we fall naturally and easily into the manner and customs which long usage has implanted ineradicably within us.

Once he left public school, Tarzan's habits were swinging from tree to tree, saving the hapless Jane and doing a spot of loincloth laundry. No girl wants to be saved by a hero who smells. The government tells us to wash our hands, but don't forget to wash your clothes. This book is not just academic!

The 1890s psychologist G. Stanley Hall, who never swung from branch to branch, had the same idea as Tarzan's creator. He wrote:

> Man is largely a creature of habit, and many of his activities are more or less automatic reflexes from the stimuli of his environment.

G. Stanley Hall was friends with John Watson, a famous psychologist who invented deodorant, which is useful when stuck at home for long periods.

We are living through the most dramatic break in our habits for over 100 years. Our world has been turned upside down, which makes creatures of habit anxious and mostly unhappy. To give us some sense of control, official agencies and the media produce a cascade of statistics on the number of people affected by the virus, deaths and how various interventions work. *The New York Times*, *The Washington Post*, *The Spectator*, the BBC, the World Health Organization and many national governments provide daily data. I have tried to cite all specific sources, but sometimes in a relatively short book it seems excessive to give the date of a newspaper article both in the text and then in the Select Bibliography. Some papers have more authors than a football team. Most remarkably, there are 12 authors for a two-page paper that covers 41 patients in Spain who were bald. I have noted just the first four and then added 'et al.', which is more than enough for readers who want to check.

The coverage, academic, journalistic and from government agencies, shows some depressing trends, which include that prescriptions for antidepressants have risen some 20%. Incidents of domestic violence have been rising too.

Charities in China, the United States and Italy all report a spike in victims reaching out to family violence hotlines and organisations. In Singapore, AWARE's Women's Helpline has seen a 33% increase in February over calls received in the same month last year. In Britain, calls to the National Domestic Abuse helpline were 25% above average in the second week of lockdown and 49% higher after three weeks. According to the *Times* and other papers, divorce lawyers are reporting they are getting more 40% more inquiries than usual.

Psychology often throws up ironies. Some personality types will relish the solitude. No more having to pretend to muck in with chatty extrovert types. No more having to pretend to be interested in football.

The virus also highlights two of our greatest fears — firstly, fear of the unknown, since the virus is mysterious. If you are imaginative or just sceptical, you may wonder if we are being told the whole truth about it. And, secondly, fear of death. Every news bulletin reports tragedies of men and women who fell ill, suffered and died rather quickly and often alone — without the comfort of children, spouses or even friends at their side. Is that going to be our fate? Nurses and other health care workers have never been so important.

The pen is mightier than the sword in some situations, but not this one.

A book cannot unmake a pandemic, but it can give help in coping and perspective. This book does not peddle the positive — Dr Pangloss, Voltaire's character who thought all was for the best in the best of all possible worlds, does not feature — but one should remember that a crisis is also often an opportunity. Cue the amazing Captain Moore, who kept walking round his garden at the age of 99; he has shown that it is never too late to do something extraordinary and worthwhile. His walk raised £32 million for the NHS.

This book looks at the history and psychology of pandemics and how to cope. Pandemics have been endemic since biblical times. Different personality types will react differently, especially to isolation. Introverts may sometimes find it easier to manage because they will feel less pressure to fit in with others than before. Extroverts will find it harder.

The book also looks at the effects of social isolation on children and family life, and economic worries. Being passive and spending hours in front of television or watching 'athletes' playing video games is not ideal.

We will also need fun to get through this. The virus should provoke much black humour, that time-honoured way of dealing with tragedy, but Sophie Scott (2020) warned in *The Psychologist*,

> I haven't seen many jokes that get beyond the frankly relatively simple humorous relationship between the name of the kind of virus and the name of a beer. Indeed, it appears that this same relationship has been enough to make the stock market lose some faith in the Corona beer brand. So maybe we are due a really excellent Coronavirus joke that can start to cheer everyone up.

It may be slow coming because, as Scott points out, we are keen to police humour nowadays and not to offend. Her partner speaks of how extremely unfunny his dad found the famous 'One leg too few' sketch by Peter Cook and Dudley Moore. "Having lost a leg at the age of 11, his dad was not especially minded to see the funny side of someone with two legs hopping around to comic effect."

His reaction is very understandable, but jokes and humour are a way of dealing with anger and hostility, and we are all bound to feel angry at times now. So this book is also a light-hearted self-help guide to coping in these strangest of times.

It is clear pandemic and post-pandemic effects will last longer than optimistic politicians – and not just President Trump – believe, even if a vaccine is developed quickly. In the UK alone, 68 million people will need to be vaccinated and there are thousands who are hostile to vaccines and fantasise they are a medical conspiracy. This book also looks at lessons we can learn from the pandemic and how it has affected and will affect human behaviour. At first many experts suggested that by October 2020 the virus' effects would be fading. Now with fears of second or even third spikes of the illness, that optimism has faded.

Before examining the science of virus, a small history detour. When he defeated the Gauls in 45 BC, the Roman Emperor Julius Caesar boasted 'Veni Vidi Vici': 'I came I saw I conquered'. It was lucky for him he did not run into Asterix and his magic potion, which enabled him to biff every Roman who came near him into unconsciousness. If the virus could speak, it might smirk and snarl imitating Caesar: 'Veni, Vidi, Viri': 'I came I saw I virused'. Freud wrote a book on jokes that stressed the value of humour and emphasised how it could help defuse anxiety. The problem is that we are lacking good jokes, and so many are shit jokes in both senses of the word. One runs 'Your COVID test came back positive', to which someone replies, 'That can't be right, I've got 300 rolls of toilet paper'. Please stop me laughing, I don't think.

Basics

Viruses don't speak or smirk of course, but they do raise questions. It is important first to know just what a virus is. Can you tell it from a bacterium or a microbe or a dendrite?

For about a century, as reported in *Scientific American* in 2018, scientists have changed their minds over what viruses are. First they were seen as poisons, then as life-forms, then as biological chemicals. Today they are placed in a grey area between living and non-living: they cannot replicate on their own but can do so in living cells and can also affect the behaviour of their 'hosts' profoundly.

In the late 19th century researchers realised that certain diseases, including rabies and foot-and-mouth, were caused by particles that seemed to behave like bacteria but were much smaller. Viruses were then thought to be the simplest of all living forms.

Tobacco changed that theory. In 1935, Wendell M. Stanley and his colleagues, at what is now The Rockefeller University in New York City, crystallised a virus into – the tobacco mosaic virus – for the first time. The tobacco virus consisted of complex biochemicals, but they were not living organisms. Stanley shared the 1946 Nobel Prize, but it was for chemistry, not medicine.

A virus may not be alive but when it enters a cell (called a host after infection), it becomes active. It sheds its coat, bares its genes and oils the cell's own replication machinery to reproduce the intruder's DNA and manufacture more viral protein. The newly created viral bits assemble and turn into more viruses. Without the raw materials and energy of the host cell the virus does not multiply and spread.

Most known viruses are innocuous and may remain dormant for long periods or take advantage of the cells' replication apparatus to reproduce at a slow and steady rate. Slow and steady is too boring for Hollywood, which has had a crush on viruses that threaten to wipe out civilisation since the cinema started.

That fear is the background to *The Seventh Seal*, Ingmar Bergman's masterpiece about a knight playing chess with death. There have also been many turkeys like *Contagion* and *The Rabies That Ate Our Street* and *Outbreak* of 1995. The plot such as it is: When a new viral disease breaks out in a small American town, scientists race against time to stop it from spreading. Unfortunately, they also have to deal with a bloodthirsty Army general who wants to use the virus as a bioweapon and is determined to prevent a cure from being found. Wolfgang Petersen 'helmed', as *Variety* always puts it, and put the gloss on this celluloid germ.

Viruses affect all life on earth, often determining what will survive. But viruses also evolve. The Nobel laureate Salvador Luria declared in 1959, "May we not feel that in the virus, in their merging with the cellular genome and re-emerging from them, we observe the units and process which, in the course of evolution, have created the successful genetic patterns that underlie all living cells?"

In the last 30 years we have seen a number of frightening viruses such as AIDS (causing HIV-1), SARS and Ebola. These may be the only biological entities that researchers can actually see come into being, providing a real-time example of evolution in action.

So the virus sneaks into cells and begins to do its damage. The virus has no psychology, but its victims do, and their reactions depend on their basic health, their psychology and money. Money matters because if you do not have the money to eat properly, you are more likely to suffer.

Get the grub in

At the start of the pandemic in the UK supermarkets shoppers were in a toilet paper frenzy. One colleague told me his wife had bought 1,600 rolls.

He was only a little embarrassed. Such panic buying has passed but it is still sensible to make sure you have the supplies you need – and a little extra. What are your essential supplies will depend on taste and on money, which is a crucial factor.

Millions who have worked and never would have dreamed of needing to use a food bank have found they have to in this crisis. The German playwright Bertolt Brecht, whose plays include *Mother Courage* and the *Resistible Rise of Arturo Ui* (a satire on Hitler's rise set in Chicago gangland), once said 'first grub then philosophy'.

In a rich country like the UK no one should go hungry, but they do. The many financial schemes the government has set seem to miss many people, including over 1 million self employed people. By 1 June 2020, 16 million Americans were unemployed as compared to 3 million at the start of the pandemic, the U.S. Bureau of Labour (2020) reported. The Chancellor of the Exchequer often preferred to use the word 'furloughed', which sounds less grim than unemployed. But any worker who is furloughed is likely to be anxious about when, and if, they will return to work.

When it comes to grub, and also social analysis, the Trussell Trust does good work. It supports a network of 1,200 food banks that "provide emergency food and support to people locked in poverty, and campaign for change to end the need for food banks in the UK" (The Trussel Trust End of Year Statistics, 2019). The Trust argues that 14 million people are living in poverty – including 4.5 million children. Their food banks provide a minimum of three days' emergency food to people in crisis. Between April 2018 and March 2019, their food banks sent 1.6 million food supplies to people in crisis, a 19% increase on the previous year. Emma Revie, its Chief Executive, said:

> As a nation we expect no one should be left hungry or destitute – illness, disability, family breakdown or the loss of a job could happen to any of us, and we owe it to each other to make sure sufficient financial support is in place when we need it most.

In America, food banks are also seeing unprecedented demands as unemployment soars to over 20 million people. Adele La Tourette, who leads the New Jersey Anti-Hunger Coalition, told me that she had not seen so many people using food banks before – and many were unexpected. They had had decent, well-paying jobs before the virus decimated the economy.

Poverty is affecting groups it has never affected before. Carlos Rodriguez, who heads a small New Jersey food bank, reported that one Wednesday in March 2020, his food bank served 1,300 casino workers and their families, who waited patiently inside their cars wrapped around Harbour Square Mall while emergency meal kits and fresh produce were loaded into their trunks. One a day in late May the drive-through distribution at Newark's Branch

Brook Park helped an additional 2,065 families; 3,365 families were served during drive-through distributions in Newark and Egg Harbour Township.

Suddenly having no job and no money is a psychological shock. Some research by Martin Seligman on dogs has made clear how feeling helpless is corrosive – and the virus and its economic impact is causing such feelings. Seligman followed the operating conditioning model of the behaviourist B.F. Skinner. Rats, pigeons and human beings are affected by the probability that their behaviour leads to a reward or punishment. Skinner famously taught pigeons to play table tennis by this method. In the first part of his experiment Seligman put three groups of dogs in a harness. In Group 1, the dogs are simply attached to their harness for a short time and then released. Groups 2 and 3 remain attached. Group 2 is given an electric shock, which the dogs can stop by pressing a lever. Each dog in Group 3 suffers a shock as long and as intense as those in Group 2, but the dogs in Group 3 cannot stop the shock. The only way for a Group 3 dog to escape the shock is for a Group 2 dog to operate its lever. Group 3 dogs could not act on their own to escape. In the end, dogs in Groups 1 and 2 recovered quickly from their experience, while dogs in Group 3 learned to be helpless and showed symptoms similar to chronic depression.

One way of combatting the anxieties provoked by the virus is to prepare for action, even if it is the kind of action you never expected to take. It gives you some control.

Be prepared if you are afraid of being unable to buy food. Research your nearest food banks, too – and how you can get food from them.

Anything that informs you (from a reliable source) is useful, as it is vital to make sense of the swirl of statistics, but they are complicated and often contradictory. Different countries record deaths in different ways. Still so far from 1 January to 1 May 2020, there seem to have been some 250,000 deaths worldwide. And there will be thousands more. Each death is a tragedy for the victims, their friends and families, but this pandemic seems to be less vicious than the Spanish flu of 1918, which killed an estimated 40 million, let alone the mediaeval Black Death. It is worth remembering our ancestors had it even worse sometimes.

This is an international crisis but there are cultural differences. As I discuss ways of coping, I know my ideas will apply most to European and American cultures. I would not presume to offer advice to cultures like India, Japan or China, but there are some events that show how when human beings are afraid, they will try the oddest remedies. Madagascar soldiers went door-to-door doling out sachets of a local herbal tea touted by President Andry Rajoelina as a remedy. COVID-Organics is a tonic derived from artemisia – a plant with proven efficacy in treating malaria. It has not been tested internationally, which did not discourage the President of Madagascar either. "This herbal tea gives results in seven days," Rajoelina announced at its official launch.

Could your health possibly be worse?

The crime writer Dorothy Sayers was all too aware of the draw of snake oil. She did not just create the toff sleuth Lord Peter Wimsey. In 1937 she wrote an essay on advertising for *The Spectator* and made fun of the way medicines played on our fears and up to our hopes. President Trump saying that bleach will kill the virus is a good example. If in this crisis Sayers were writing the government copy, which would make it easier to read, as she was a brilliant copywriter, it might go something like this:

Do you have heart disease, diabetes 1, diabetes 2, any other form of diabetes yet to be discovered, indeed any disease yet to be discovered since doctors don't know it all?

If you're not diabetic, do you suffer from kidney failure, liver failure because you've swigged too much booze like Guinness. [Sayers wrote the famous ad 'Guinness is good for you'.]

Are your lungs fit for purpose? Why not buy your own personal back up?

When did you last have a headache? How would you rate it on a scale where 3 is 'get me a whisky fast' and 9 is 'hand me that sledgehammer so I can knock myself out'?

Then get on those scales. Are you overweight or, be honest, seriously overweight or frankly obese? Oh dear, oh dear, you thought you were just a bit podgy.

The letter from the Homerton Hospital I got after the one from Downing Street was enough to provoke an acute anxiety attack. It clarified the government guidance. It told me to keep up to date with the latest online info as I fall into the group of those who have to be 'particularly stringent' in following social distancing measures for two reasons: I am over 70 and I have an underlying health condition. My GP insisted I attend outpatients to have my right leg scanned as it was very painful – which might be a warning sign of worse things.

I was whisked off to the Homerton and X-rayed. Luckily there were no tell-tale lesions, which are a symptom of myeloma, cancer of the blood. I have to be monitored every three months because the symptoms have the nasty habit of suddenly hitting you without advance warning – and then I would need chemotherapy. I was all-clear. I had none of the symptoms of the virus either – no dry cough, no fever, no dizziness. Great; well, not so great. The medical profession did not know why my leg hurt, which was not reassuring. Sciatica was a guess . . . maybe or maybe not. Not knowing has left me worried that the unknown malady will come back. I decided to call my condition 'Leg not quite in irons'.

The official letters I received did not mention mental health, but the virus and isolation are bound to add to stress and cause problems. As this is an unprecedented event, there are aspects which cry out for research. One is visual. As I look out of my window in mid-afternoon, the streets look strange because they are empty. In about two minutes there is only a white van driving past. The cafes are closed. The virus has wiped the world clean and green. It has reduced emissions significantly. Two new studies in *Geophysical Research Letters* reported by Lipuma (2020) found nitrogen dioxide pollution over northern China, Western Europe and the US decreased by as much as 60% in early 2020 as compared to the same time in 2019. Typically, nitrogen dioxide is produced by emissions from vehicles, power plants and industrial activities. 'Particulate matter pollution' (particles smaller than 2.5 microns) has decreased by 35% in northern China (Bauwens et al., 2020). These particles and liquid droplets are small enough to penetrate deep into the lungs and cause damage. Coronavirus means many of us can breathe better. Ambitious academics should get cracking on the PhDs now – the look, smells and sounds of a changed world.

Isolation is difficult, but living in the presence of your family 24/7 in too small a space is also hard. The housing charity Shelter offers a complicated set of equations about overcrowding, using a method called the space standard. There are two ways to work out if a home is overcrowded under current law using this method.

First count the number of people:

- anyone aged 10 or over counts as 1 person
- children aged 1 to 9 count as 0.5
- children under 1 year old don't count

Next, count the number of rooms or measure the floor space of each room. Don't count any room that is:

- under 50 square feet or 4.6 square metres
- not a bedroom or living room

Shelter offers the example of a couple with two boys aged 16 and 11 and a girl aged 17 who live in a three-bedroom flat with a living room. They aren't overcrowded under the room standard because 7.5 people are allowed to live in a home with four rooms under these rules.

But if all four rooms are less than 69 square feet, the family is overcrowded under the space standard, because under these rules only 0.5 people should sleep in a room of that size. A room must be 110 square feet for two people to live in it.

Inevitably, with more of us being confined than ever before, people are turning to meds and more meds. In May 2020, Express Scripts, a pharmacy benefit management program, found that the use of prescription drugs to treat mental health conditions increased more than 20% between mid-February and mid-March, peaking the week of 15 March, when the World Health Organization declared COVID-19 a pandemic. Prescriptions for anti-anxiety medications rose 34%, while prescriptions for antidepressants increased by 18%, according to Ao in March 2020.

"We're using antidepressants more and more to treat both anxiety and depression," according to Michael Liebowitz, a professor of clinical psychiatry at Columbia University, reported in *MedicalXpress* on 28 April 2020 (Ao, 2020). He called the pandemic "a huge added stress factor", saying that it has made coping incredibly difficult for people vulnerable to anxiety and depression. Overuse of medication will be one of its legacies.

Liebowitz did not mention that other cause of vulnerability – other people.

'Hell is other people'

The 20th century French philosopher Jean-Paul Sartre said this in his play *Huis Clos*, where three people are locked in a room. Unhappily. A loves B, B loves C and C loves A. Hardly a recipe for a happy ending. In real life Sartre was gregarious and, despite a long-standing relationship with Simone de Beauvoir, was apt to leap into bed with students who thought he was brilliant.

Our lives are ruled by our relations with other people – wives, husbands, children, lovers, bosses. Without such drama as *Huis Clos* all these relationships are under pressure as a result of coronavirus. The trick is to make being with other people as easy as possible.

The question of space is vital – and space again is often a question of money. If you live with your partner in a semi-detached house with a garden, you have plenty of chances to be together and also to be apart – both essentials in this situation. If you live in a small, two-bedroom flat with no outside space, that will be much harder and avoiding tensions and rows will be more important. Talking about the changed structure of your day is a start.

When structure changes

Human beings like structure. We wake up, we have breakfast with family (or most of us do), we go to work, we plan what we'll do at the weekend when we don't have to be constrained by the normal.

We don't have these certainties now.

And we have no idea when we will have them again.

But our biology can be a help. The brain likes new experiences, as we shall see. Pamper your cortex by taking the opportunity to try something new.

The lockdown is also an unprecedented experiment as millions of us have to live in ways we have never lived before. Freud, who lived through the terrors of the 1914 war and the Spanish flu epidemic, said humankind created religion to cope with uncertainty. If you prayed hard enough to the right gods, the volcano would not blow, the storm would abate, the crops would grow. Recent research partly supports the hope we invest in religion. In the United States a March 2020 survey carried out by the Pew Research Centre showed that 24% of people said their faith has gotten stronger as the virus spread. The group with the largest number of respondents who said their faith has got stronger is black Protestants, at 56% – and they tended to be poor (Gecewicz, 2020).

In writing this book, I also decided to carry out a small experiment.

There are 35 people in my usual but now out-of-physical-touch world. I talk to most of them two or three times a week. Obviously this is not a random sample, as I know them. I have kept them anonymous. My friend M, for example, is very anxious about her 90-year-old mother and fears she may never see her again. Her cousin W has daughter who is a nurse and is terrified she will catch the virus and die.

P's two teenage children have been continuing with school remotely and P has kept busy with work. Her father is petrified of catching the virus.

N is becoming obsessed with the virus and what to do to avoid it. If he had his way everyone would gorge on supplements and vitamins and do breathing exercises 24/7. Love and anxiety go hand in hand. N's mother lives far away and is missing him. There is real anxiety in the town. Two people in her terrace have been stricken. She orders food online but worries about whether to risk going to the local convenience store to buy papers. The local greengrocer has taken to wearing a mask and gloves. N's aunt is divorcing her husband, but he can't move out of their small house during the crisis, so they are forced into unwanted proximity.

Just before the lockdown, a long-ago lover of mine, H, went away with friends for a holiday. The holiday was cut short, but they managed to get back on the last plane home. H has offered to lend me money as she fears that I will run short as Airbnb, one source of my income, has dried up.

My filmmaking colleague D is locked in an edit suite where he also sleeps. He is trying to finish a film. His problem is a common one – trying not to drink too much because is isolated.

G is 80-plus and struggling to cope with her disabled daughter; she drives 50 miles to Wales twice a week to look after her. Her husband was in a care home at the start of the pandemic, but she could not see him. That upset both of them. Then he died alone. She was rung by the care home to inform her and then she had to cope with his death from the virus on her own.

An author whose rom-com book I have promised to publish has been sacked from her job and came back home only for her relationship to break up.

E is off sick with poor kidney function. His hopes of a transplant are gone for the present. He and his wife are also going through IVF for the second time, which is hard on them both. E's sister has just given birth. Her partner has just been told his pay is being cut by 20%. Like many, the virus is making them struggle financially. She had to borrow £20 to get a lamb roast for Easter dinner.

My rabbi's dog who she loves has started to bite her, which she finds upsetting.

All these friends have agreed about what makes them anxious, what makes them afraid and how they spend their time.

As this book has personal elements, I will also report on my interactions with my GP, which are frustrating when you can only consult him by phone. How can he diagnose what is wrong with my leg, which still hurts, when he can't examine it? I'm not in danger but it bothers me. When doctors cannot see you, it causes more uncertainty. And if you do go to a hospital for an X-ray, you worry you will catch the virus. I will analyse the responses of my 35 associates in a later chapter.

Chapter 1

Anxiety and the brain
Taking control of your fears

Our brain consumes 20% of the oxygen we use. The brain is busy and needs to be busy while we are awake. It likes both puzzles and answers. The latter are in short supply at present as the virus baffles the best scientific brains.

Psychologists make much of the concept of 'free-floating anxiety' to which some kinds of personalities are prone. Traditionally it means being anxious without having a specific reason for it. Today, anxiety all too easily free floats and makes you worry about how soon you will catch the virus, what will you do then, the hospitals won't take you and you'll be die in appalling pain. Your family won't be there, and the overworked undertakers will put you at the back of the queue: "We'll find him a spot someday. Meanwhile put him in Fridge 27 and check no one left sardines in there."

I have deliberately added the disgusting sardine detail to suggest that you shouldn't let anxiety kill your sense of humour.

On 19 May 2020 *The Lancet* published a review which analysed 65 studies of patients who had been treated in hospital for SARS, MERS and coronavirus. The samples were international. A third of those who had suffered from MERS and SARS went on to develop post-traumatic stress disorder, so the evidence suggests the coronavirus will affect some of us for a long time.

The Lancet paper also reported that worrying a lot about whether you had MERS or SARS correlated with poorer mental health in the long run – and health care workers had the worst mental health outcomes.

University College London (2020) is conducting a weekly survey of responses to the crisis. Its findings give a sense of the national mood. Its Virus Watch has surveyed 42,500 people. The 21 May results include that compliance with government advice has decreased since lockdown began, moving from an average of 70% of adults 'completely' adhering to just 60%. Confidence in government has fallen slightly since the start of lockdown and is lowest in those under the age of 30.

Anxiety levels have fallen further, although depression levels remain relatively stable. Both appear higher than usual reported averages.

Stress relating to COVID-19 (both catching COVID-19 and becoming seriously ill from COVID-19) has stabilised again following a rise, with 1 in 5 people now worried about it.

Thoughts of death or self-harm and experience of self-harm or abuse remain relatively stable but are higher amongst younger people and those living alone, with low household income, with a mental health condition and living in urban areas. Levels reported here are expected to be underestimations of experiences. Loneliness levels continue to be stable since lockdown started, even amongst high-risk groups. Levels are higher in women, people living with children and people living in urban areas.

Fifty percent of respondents do not currently feel in control of future plans, while 39% do not feel in control of their employment and 23% do not feel in control of their mental health. When comparing across age groups, younger adults report feeling less in control across all domains. Seventy-eight percent are concerned about cases of COVID-19 increasing as lockdown is eased, and 74% are concerned about people not adhering to social distancing. The most prevalent factors people are missing from their normal lives are meeting up with friends (81%) and family (77%). One in three people are missing having time on their own. Overall, younger adults are more worried than any other group.

The amygdala

One of the brain structures that is central to anxiety is the amygdala, whose name comes from the Latin for 'almond'. It forms part of what is sometimes called the emotional brain. The amygdala increases its activity in response to isolation and affects fear and anxiety, symptoms prisoners in solitary confinement often suffer.

Some very recent work – admittedly in mice – offers the eventual prospect of helping people control their anxiety. Bertero, Feyen, Zurita and Apicella from the University of Texas at San Antonio have just published 'A non-canonical cortico-amygdala inhibitory loop' in the 2020 *Journal of Neuroscience*. Conditions such as post-traumatic stress, anxiety and depression are thought to be linked to the abnormal functioning of the amygdala.

The research "provides anatomical and physiological evidence for the existence of a long-range inhibitory pathway from the auditory cortex to the amygdala in the mouse brain", Apicella and colleagues said. "For the first time, in our paper we show this emotional pathway." He added that the inhibitory cortical neurons can alter the activity of the amygdala's principal neurons and can therefore directly control the output of the amygdala. The neurons contain somatostatin, which regulates physiological functions and forms a connection with principal neurons that project to other brain regions outside the amygdala that are involved in fear and aversive behaviour.

"The discovery that the amygdala receives both excitatory and inhibitory inputs from that cortex suggests that the timing and relative strength of these inputs can affect the activity of the amygdala," the researchers said. Excitatory neurotransmitters have excitatory effects on the neuron. This means they increase the likelihood that the neuron will fire an action potential. Inhibitory neurotransmitters have inhibitory effects on the neuron.

Apicella and his research team noted that future experiments should examine whether this is a general mechanism by which sensory stimuli can influence the processes controlled by the amygdala, such as fear/aversive behaviour and anxiety. The intriguing possibility – far off and very speculative – is that some noises might help calm anxiety. Some music certainly does for some people.

The practical hint from this is try to find music or even birdsong – there is plenty on Google – which soothes you.

This research is welcome as there are no easy ways to master anxiety, but that does not mean we are helpless. First and crucially, know your anxieties. You will find some easy to identify, but try to winkle out the ones you are ashamed of. One obvious example: If you live with someone, shouldn't that be a great for a love fest or sex romp? Yet many relationships won't work that way. George Bernard Shaw defined marriage as the maximum of opportunity with the minimum of temptation.

Keep a record

One useful habit to acquire as our habits change is to keep a diary. In 1980, psychologist E.J. Dearnley gave a paper in which he reported how he spent his time, day and night. He bought a buzzer which went off at random times day and he jotted down what he was doing when the buzzer went off. Over a year, Dearnley discovered he spent much of his time working at his desk, some of it grooming himself and a considerable amount of time in what he called leisure. Leisure had little to do with physical fitness, though. Dearnley's main leisure activity was drinking in one of the many locales near him. He would really suffer today, as at the time of writing, pubs and restaurants are still closed even though lockdown has eased. But note how much of each day you spent in activities other than work, looking after children, sleeping and grooming. Try to spend 90 minutes at least on some kind of relaxation.

Keeping track of how you do will give you a sense of achievement if you do well.

Practical steps:

Open a page for each day
Record your anxieties – see below for sources of anxiety
Record your feelings – the ups and the downs
In the morning, if you remember them, record your dreams
Record the exercises you have done

Note how well you do each of them when you start
Add any comments about how you feel about doing them
Choose what you feel is your favourite exercise
Be honest about days when you skive off, can't be bothered to think or do
fewer exercises than normal

When you write a list you impose an element of control. After all, you are doing the writing. So list what makes you anxious, what makes you irritated, what makes you feel you are coping and what makes you happy. As the situation provokes anxiety, let's start there.

Each one of us will have anxieties we would rather not face, but be brave and list your anxieties. Some obvious ones:

Feeling abandoned if you are self-isolating
Feeling crowded if you are cooped up with your family
Feeling you don't like one of your children
Feeling unhappy because of the tensions in your relationship
Feeling stressed because you are not at work
Feeling stressed because you are out of work
Feeling worried about money
Feeling disturbed by your dreams
Feeling inadequate

These are just general headings. This is not some idiosyncratic idea of mine. Psychotherapists of every ilk – and there are ilks and ilks of them belonging to different schools who often don't get on well because they seem steeped in rivalries about whose theory is top – agree with Freud, who believed, in effect, that to be is to be anxious. His death principle stated that one reason we sometimes fantasise about death is that then we won't feel any anxiety. It's a nice theory, but hardly a way to cope.

Sometimes I think psychoanalysis should have a theme song and there is an obvious candidate: "I Can't Get No Satisfaction".

Over 30 years Freud's views on anxiety changed. At first he blamed sexual frustration. Unsatisfied libido became toxic and transformed into anxiety. Freud often warned his patients against excessive masturbation, which did not satisfy libidos that wanted the real thing. In *Three Essays on the Theory of Sexuality* (1953), he said, "neurotic anxiety arises out of libido, and is thus related to it in the same kind of way as vinegar is to wine."

Then he developed his theory of repression. Repression is, as the word suggests, keeping down ideas connected to sexual desire and keeping then out of consciousness when they conflict with 'civilised' social norms. He widened the causes of anxiety so that it was now caused not just by a failure to get satisfaction, but also by psychological inhibitions.

In the late 1920s, Freud changed his ideas again. He argued we were all prone to automatic anxiety, triggered by a traumatic situation in which the helpless ego is overwhelmed. These 'danger situations' are triggered by the threats of losing a loved one or of being attacked. Avoiding anxiety was part of the essential work of the mind.

In the late 1930s Freud made an enemy of a young psychiatrist because he did not reply when Viktor Frankl sent him a paper he had written and asked for his opinion of it. Frankl accosted him on the street and Freud said he had no idea who he was. Frankl was hurt and developed logotherapy as an alternative to psychoanalysis. Your libido is not the problem nor is your complex. Your problem is that you need to feel you have meaning in your life. And if you don't feel you have this, Frankl's therapy would provide ideas for you to build on. In the 1970s I interviewed him about his split with Freud (which certainly gave his life meaning) and the technique of paradoxical intention he devised. It offers a way of dealing with anxiety.

Identify what makes you anxious first. Then imagine that and make yourself more and more anxious about it. Let's say you are phobic about cats – then imagine you are surrounded by cats. And more cats. And cats climbing all over you. Frankl claimed with some evidence that repeating this would make it easier for you to cope with cats.

Paradoxical intention is thought to be ideal for insomnia, particularly where there is intense preoccupation about sleep, sleep loss and its consequences. The paradox is that the patient who cannot sleep is told to stay awake as long as possible. The instruction is intended to reduce anxiety at bedtime (Ascher and Turner, 1979). Some controlled studies have found paradoxical intention to be effective for when people find it hard to fall asleep (e.g., Ascher and Turner, 1979; Espie et al., 1989) but others have not (Lacks et al., 1983; Turner and Ascher, 1982). Here is the paradox. Instructing the patient to stay awake should increase a sense of voluntary control over sleep (Bateson et al., 1956), because if one successfully follows the paradoxical intention, one will gain control over sleep by 'not sleeping'. Mixed results, but the technique is worth trying. If you take sleeping pills and you don't drift off, you may be tempted to take more, which is dangerous. You can't overdose on paradoxical intention, though.

Frankl was a fine climber and his office was decorated with pictures of himself on top of various mountains in the Alps. He knew about breathing as a result, and one of the lessons of this crisis is to focus on breathing. If you have coronavirus with any severity, you struggle to breathe, which is painful. If you don't, you still need to breathe and think about breathing because deep breathing relaxes both body and mind.

You do not have to practice yoga to breathe properly and to devote two 15-minute sessions a day to focus on your breathing. Breathe in, suck the breath down deep, breathe out slowly. This takes practice and concentration.

I tend to do this in the bath, breathing in and out 25 times. It starts off being irritating and boring but after eight or ten breaths I get into some kind of rhythm and my mind empties of everything, so for a little while nothing makes me feel anxious.

Frankl worked in Vienna, where the medical practice of hand washing originated. In the 19th century most doctors did not realise that poor hygiene could kill their patients. Then a Hungarian doctor named Philipp Semmelweis discovered that the incidence of puerperal fever (also known as 'childbed fever') could be drastically cut by the use of hand disinfection in maternity wards. In 1847 he proposed washing hands with chlorinated lime solutions while working in Vienna General Hospital's first obstetrical clinic, where doctors' wards had three times the mortality of midwives' wards. Wards where hands were washed reduced mortality to below 1%, but doctors dismissed his ideas. Semmelweis could offer no scientific explanation for his findings. Some doctors were also offended by his suggestion that they should wash their hands and mocked him.

In 1865 Semmelweis suffered a nervous breakdown and was committed to an asylum by his colleague. He died 14 days later, at the age of 47, of gangrene, after being beaten by the asylum guards. It was only 20 years after his death that doctors began to follow basic rules of hygiene.

So, wash your hands, perhaps while saying 'Philipp Semmelweis' as a tribute rather than 'Happy Birthday'. We can learn through the virus. Research on the value of handwashing was published online on 10 December 2010 in *The Lancet* and is compiled in a comprehensive World Health Organization report on the burden of endemic health-care-associated infection worldwide.

But hand washing is also a common symptom of obsessive compulsive disorder, as is repeatedly checking things (oven turned off, door locked, etc.) that a person associates with harm or danger. Some people are afraid that if everything isn't perfect or done just right, something terrible will happen, or they will be punished. Professor Craig Jackson, writing in *The Psychologist* on 17 March 2020, suggested that:

> there is a possible danger that the current uncertainty around COVID-19 could make things worse for those with obsessive-type conditions. For those with OCD or conditions involving cleanliness, neatness, germphobia, tidiness or some obsessive behaviours, the COVID-19 outbreak may actually reinforce to them that their problem-behaviours were actually what kept them safe during the outbreak. This could make their conditions even harder to treat or manage in the future.

He suggests trying to avoid panicking as then we lose the ability to take control:

> If we are able to replace doubt and worry caused by uncertainty, with knowledge and fact and sensible interpretations of media stories, we may

cope better and be in a better place for making rational decisions, not just for ourselves, but for others we know who may not be able to do so.

At the end of each day, note how your anxieties have fared. Examine the record, because one way to keep a sense of control is not to rely just on memory but on a written record so you can track your moods and thoughts. You will then be giving yourself a kind of narrative therapy – a form of psychotherapy – which should allow you to identify and live your values, follow how your feelings have changed and use these values to confront your problems.

Chapter 2

The effects of solitude
Case studies in isolation

Greta Garbo famously was said to have said, "I want to be alone." She clarified that she actually did not even say "I want to be left alone" but that "I want to be let alone."

My own experience of being let alone by my parents taught me that it was painful, but I coped – mainly by taking long walks and also by working hard at my school work. I learned more than any Jewish boy should about the ideas of Luther, Calvin and the more obscure Zwingli.

In the current situation over 1.2 million people are 'shielded' and are advised to stay alone with no contact with others. Food will be delivered to their door and they can talk to their doctors, but human contact is discouraged, if not quite illegal. Lord Sumption, a fine judge, has argued this infringes our civil liberties, but I have been compliant. *The Lancet* recently published a review of the psychological impact of quarantine which highlighted "negative psychological effects including post-traumatic stress symptoms, confusion, and anger. Stressors included longer quarantine duration, infection fears, frustration, boredom, inadequate supplies, inadequate information, financial loss, and stigma" (Brooks et al., 2020).

Saints and hermits often spent years alone in caves, or in the case of the somewhat exhibitionistic Simeon Stylites, on top of a pillar in the desert. People came to the bottom of the pillar to visit him so he was not that alone, but he was part of a spiritual tradition. Many 'holy' women and men have claimed that being alone brings them closer to God.

My friend Sara Maitland (2009), the writer and theologian, has written of her life in solitude in southeast Scotland:

> I didn't seek solitude, it sought me. It evolved gradually after my marriage broke down. I found myself living on my own in a small country village. At first I was miserable and cross. It took me between six months and a year before I noticed that I had become phenomenally happy. And this was about being alone – not about being away from my husband. I found out, for instance, how much I liked being in my garden. My subconscious was cleverer than my conscious in choosing to live alone. The discovery about solitude was a surprise in waiting.

Maitland suggests we need to read about the lives of solitaries who have enjoyed it, to take it on and see what is good in it.

Hermits rarely climb to the top of the greasy pole. The great exception was Pope Celestine V (1215–1296). Before being manipulated by various cardinals into becoming what historians call an 'appalling' and 'inglorious' Pope, he slept in a cave on bare rock and practised mortification of the flesh, wearing horsehair shirts and an iron girdle. He was forced out of his hermitage and into the papacy in 1292 at the age of 84. He quit after five months. After his failed term as Pope, Celestine wanted to return to his 'tranquil' life as a hermit but was instead thrown in jail by his successor over fears that he might become an antipope, or rival.

Celestine presumably never went to a brothel; a rather more worldly solitary was Valerio Ricetti (1898–1952), who moved to Australia in 1914 at age 16 after an uncle loaned him money to escape the 1914 war. He worked in the mines and lived for a short time with an Italian family before losing all of his money in a brothel (he didn't spend it, he literally lost it). He then found what he called his 'Garden of Eden' in a cave near the town of Griffith and decided to live in the wild. He built a house, gardens and even a little 'chapel' that he painted with Christian imagery. He lived in the cave for roughly 23 years before being placed in an internment camp when Italy entered World War II in 1940.

The third hermit of note, Maxime Qavtaradze, is a 63-year-old Georgian monk who lives at the top of the Katskhi Pillar, a 130-foot-tall limestone rock used by Christian ascetics until the 15th century when the Ottoman Empire invaded. He began his new life in 1993 and only comes down from the pillar once or twice a week. He slept inside a refrigerator for the first two years to protect himself from the elements. He now lives in a small cottage on the pillar that local Christians helped him build. It takes him about 20 minutes to climb down a ladder to the small religious community at the base of the pillar that formed after Qavtaradze decided to take up residence on his rock.

In literature there are heroes and heroines who have to spend years alone. Defoe based his Robinson Crusoe on the real experiences of the Scottish pirate Alexander Selkirk, who was marooned on the rather lovely island of Juan Fernandez 400 miles off the coast of Chile. Pirates often fell out.

Selkirk raised goats, farmed and every day climbed to the highest point on the island to look for signs of a ship that might rescue him. It's a tough climb, as I did it myself when filming a series on pirates. In 1994 you could still visit the hut he built as a shelter.

Selkirk was rescued after four years, got back to Scotland in 1709 and told Defoe his story. He recovered well from his isolation. It seems likely that this was because he was not helpless on the island but very active physically. Helplessness aggravates the problems of isolation, especially for those in prison or psychiatric hospitals.

Solitary confinement has been used as a punishment for centuries. In the 1970s the Soviet Union often used it to punish dissidents. In the American penal system it is still frequent. In secure psychiatric facilities temporary solitary is often used as a punishment. The cases that follow are extreme, but they show what human beings can endure and bounce back from.

Before turning to the very considerable research on the damage isolation can cause, it is worth reporting a positive recent study.

Some scholars believe that spending time alone can be good for creativity, self-insight, self-development, relaxation and spirituality if you are spending time alone out of choice. Virginia Thomas and Margarita Azmitia (2019) studied the importance of different reasons for being alone in research published in the *Journal of Adolescence* in 2019.

They created a scale measuring reasons for and attitudes to solitude. They gave it to 176 adolescents (high school students, average age of 16) and 258 young adults (college students, ages 18–25). The subjects were asked to complete the sentence, "When I spend time alone, I do so because . . ." and then indicate the importance of each of 14 reasons.

The positive reasons for being alone included

- I enjoy the quiet.
- I can engage in activities that really interest me.
- I value the privacy.
- It helps me stay in touch with my feelings.
- Being alone helps me get in touch with my spirituality.

The negative ones included

- I feel anxious when I'm with others.
- I don't feel liked when I'm with others.
- I can't be myself around others.
- I regret things I say or do when I'm with others.

Thomas and Azmitia predicted the results would be very different for the young people who spent time alone for positive reasons compared to those who did so for negative reasons.

For both the adolescents and the young adults, spending time alone for positive reasons had very little to do with loneliness. The correlation between loneliness and wanting to be alone for positive reasons was close to zero. For the young adults, spending time alone for positive reasons also had nothing to do with social anxiety or depression.

Thomas and Azmitia (2019) speculated that "low mood may drive adolescents to seek solitude to gain insight into their thoughts and feelings." Other research suggests that adolescents who spend time alone by choice feel less depressed. Perhaps feeling down motivates some adolescents to spend time alone, and they use that time effectively to regulate their mood.

The results were different and troubling for those who chose to be alone for negative reasons. They were more likely to experience loneliness and depression. These young adults were also more socially anxious.

Individuals who were alone for negative reasons were especially unlikely to have other positive experiences. They were much less likely to have positive relationships with other people or to have a clear idea about their futures. They hesitated over what jobs they wanted to do, for example. They scored low on autonomy, too.

This research is correlational. It does not tell us, for example, whether depression causes people to want to spend time alone for negative reasons, or whether the reverse is true, or whether some other factor causes people to be depressed *and* to want to spend time alone for negative reasons. Nevertheless, the results explain why some people worry about those who spend a lot of time alone. Solitude-seekers may, in fact, be feeling lonely, anxious and depressed if they choose to be alone, because they don't think other people like them, they feel like they are always saying the wrong thing or they can't be themselves when they are with other people.

For many people who choose to be alone, it's a choice at a particular time. They relish the quiet and the privacy, getting in touch with their feelings and doing things they like. They seem to be at no special risk for feeling lonely or anxious. Instead, they may be more likely to enjoy greater self-acceptance and personal growth.

Psychological damage

Most research on isolation, however, highlights the damage it can cause. Yet prisons and psychiatric hospitals often use it when they cannot control inmates or as a punishment.

Broadmoor is Britain's famous 'special hospital' for dangerous mentally ill patients. It opened in 1861 when a regime called 'moral treatment' was influential. Patients were not usually in chains and were treated relatively decently. Over time, however, the hospital became horribly overcrowded. In the early 1980s, 80 patients shared one dormitory and the nurses got used to running a punitive regime. Solitary became a form of punishment. I talked to 33 ex-patients who had been in the hospital when I made the ITV film *I Was in Broadmoor*. They complained of ill treatment often. Patients who were difficult were put in a cell with a mattress and nothing else.

One of those I talked to was 28-year-old Adrian from North London. He had not actually committed any crime – in the 1970s, you could be sent to Broadmoor if normal psychiatric hospitals could not manage you. He was upset when he was isolated, usually because he got angry with staff. He told me he tried to keep fit in isolation by doing exercises that tired him out and added that if you had not been disturbed before being put in isolation, the experience soon made you that.

There have been many reforms at Broadmoor in the last 20 years, but the British penal system still uses isolation. In 2019 Aylesbury Young Offender Institution in Buckinghamshire was severely criticised. It houses 440 inmates aged between 19 and 21 and keeps some of them in its segregation unit for up to three months at a stretch. That means they are in solitary confinement 23 hours a day. In the *Bucks Herald* on 12 September 2019, Thomas Bamford reported that the practice raised "significant concerns for their mental and physical wellbeing". The prisons and probation Ombudsman upheld complaints on behalf of three inmates who had been segregated or locked in their cells.

Many described "feeling bored, frustrated and sometimes even suicidal". The Ombudsman said:

> They often have no idea when their isolation will be brought to an end, adding to their sense of hopelessness. We have had to make numerous complaints and safeguarding referrals to the prison, which appears to be in a perpetual state of crisis.

The Ombudsman concluded:

> It is well known that locking energetic young men in their cells for excessive periods of time can cause irreversible harm. It is unfair on them and the staff charged with their care and does nothing to help prevent reoffending.

Abandoned – the trauma of being held hostage

Being held hostage is an extreme and frightening form of isolation. It has been much studied in the UK since the Spaghetti House siege. In 1979 I made an ITV film on terrorism in Holland, where trains had been hijacked by South Moluccans who felt the Dutch government had reneged on promises to them. I tracked down 33 of those who had been held hostage; 31 complained bitterly that they felt they had been abandoned by their government who did nothing to resolve the terrifying situation they found themselves in for 13 days. Three of the hostages were executed during that period. One of Holland's leading psychiatrists, Dr Bastiaans, claimed all the hostages would suffer trauma as a result of their experiences. Most did, but two men found being held hostage gave them a kind of authority they had never had before. It is important to remember how individual responses are.

The Dutch hostages' experiences were terrifying but short lived. That is very different from the experiences of some American offenders. Robert

King was in solitary confinement for 29 years. He described his experience to the Society for Neuroscience in November 2018 (Lobel and Akil, 2018). King knew that solitary confinement was changing the way his brain worked. When he finally left his cell, he realised he had trouble recognising faces. He said he had to retrain his eyes to learn what a face was like. His sense of direction was also messed up, and he was unable to follow a simple route in the city by himself. His brain had wiped out everything that it did not need to survive in a cell no bigger than the back of a pick-up truck.

One of the most remarkable effects of chronic social isolation is the decrease in the size of the hippocampus, a brain region involved in learning, memory and spatial awareness.

Studies on mice by Apicella and colleagues (2019) have shown that one month of social isolation caused a decrease of around 20% in the volume of neurons; though the brain compensated at first, the remaining neurons were branching out more than those of mice that were not isolated. After three months of isolation the extra branching of the neurons as an attempt to compensate for the trauma of isolation stopped. The brain could only try to compensate for so long.

It has been argued that solitary confinement is closer to torture and should be banned. There is much academic support for that.

In 2014, a National Academies of Science committee reviewed the existing research and concluded that solitary confinement can precipitate serious psychological change in prisoners and that the practice "is best minimized" (Travis et al., 2014, p. 201). The American Psychological Association (2016) agreed that:

> solitary confinement is associated with severe harm to physical and mental health among both youth and adults, including: increased risk of self-mutilation, and suicidal ideation; greater anxiety, depression, sleep disturbance, paranoia, and aggression; exacerbation of the onset of pre-existing mental illness and trauma symptoms; [and] increased risk of cardiovascular problems.

Similarly, the National Commission on Correctional Health Care (Camp Camille and Resnik, 2016) warned that long periods in solitary, by which they meant more than 15 days (which is nothing compared to King's experience in solitary), represents "cruel, inhumane, and degrading treatment" that is "harmful to an individual's health" (p. 260) and that health care staff must advocate to remove persons from solitary confinement whenever "their medical or mental health deteriorates" (p. 261).

Yet no one knows how many prisoners are held in solitary. One estimate for the US is 80,000. In the Soviet Union the statistics are likely to be as extreme.

A joint 2016 statement of the Association of State Correctional Administrators (the largest professional association of American prison administrators;

Camp Camille and Resnik, 2016) and Yale Law School's Liman Public Interest Program observed that demands for change in use of solitary confinement are being made around the world. But even countries with liberal regimes like Holland still make use of it.

The research suggests clearly that even 15 days in isolation is likely to affect your mental health. There are ways to mitigate this. Regularly talk to other people on the phone. Since stress can make one forgetful, set up regular times to chat – and make an effort to do more than check in with a mechanical "Are you okay?" Other research suggests that establishing a routine can help as it reduces uncertainty and facilitates a sense of control. Dr Nathan Smith and Professor Emma Barrett (2020) also make the point that "it is almost inevitable that at some point during isolation and quarantine people will experience feelings of low mood and a lack of motivation." They add this is not unusual for people living in ICE (isolated, confined and extreme) conditions, such as astronauts or submariners. In Tom Clancy's well-researched *The Hunt for Red October*, the crew of the sub cannot wait till they dock in Havana. After weeks in the deep, they are desperate for cigars and women.

Knowing that it is perfectly normal for mood and motivation to ebb and flow, with some good days and some bad days, can be comforting. Ways of coping with low mood and motivation in ICE conditions include acknowledging progress and focusing on small achievements to help foster a sense of competence.

Small strategies do help.

Chapter 3

Plagues through history
The past and its lessons for us

They had it even worse in the past, which is worth remembering. Signs of smallpox appear on 12th-century BC Egyptian mummies. In the 6th century AD the Plague of Justinian moved along trade routes, killing 25 million people across Asia, Africa, Arabia and Europe.

The Black Death spread across Europe between 1346 and 1353. In Florence, the great Renaissance poet Petrarch was sure that in the future no one would believe their suffering: "O happy posterity, who will not experience such abysmal woe and will look upon our testimony as a fable." A Florentine chronicler, di Coppa Stefani (cited in Benedictow, 2008), detailed the suffering:

> All the citizens did little else except to carry dead bodies to be buried. . . . At every church they dug deep pits down to the water-table; and thus those who were poor who died during the night were bundled up quickly and thrown into the pit. In the morning when a large number of bodies were found in the pit, they took some earth and shovelled it down on top of them; and later others were placed on top of them and then another layer of earth, just as one makes lasagne with layers of pasta and cheese.

The Black Death was an epidemic of bubonic plague, caused by the bacterium *Yersinia pestis* that circulates among wild rodents. Humans get the disease when rodents (normally black rats) become infected. The infection takes three to five days to incubate in people before they fall ill, and another three to five days before, in 80% of the cases, the victims die.

We speak of global interconnectedness as if it were new. It's not. The Black Death was spread by rat fleas on ships. Fleas don't like the cold, so the plague was a summer epidemic. In the history of Norway, from the start of the Black Death in 1348–1349 to the last outbreaks in 1654, there was never a winter epidemic.

It used to be thought that the Black Death originated in China, but new research shows that it began in the spring of 1346 in the steppes near the Caspian Sea, in Genghis Khan's territory. The epidemic began when the Mongols attacked the Italian merchants' last trading station in the Crimea. Plague broke out among the besiegers and got into the town. When spring arrived, the Italians fled on their ships – and the Black Death sailed with them.

In those God-fearing times, everyone believed the plague to be a punishment from God for their sins. They responded with religious fervour or sometimes with passivity and fatalism. If God wishes the plague on you, you better go along with it, as it was a sin to try to avoid God's will.

Rats and their fleas were first-class sailors. The voyage of a ship from Bordeaux in 1348 is worth following. Around 8 May it reached Melcombe Regis, near Weymouth in Dorset; the epidemic broke out shortly before 24 June. Bristol was contaminated in June; London was hit in early August and the Black Death spread inland. All of England was afflicted in the course of 1349. Iceland and Finland were the only regions that avoided the Black Death because they had tiny populations with minimal contact with other countries.

Researchers used to agree that the Black Death killed 20–30% of Europe's population, but from 1960, new mortality studies from various parts of Europe were published. It is now clear that the earlier estimates of mortality should be doubled. Two facts stand out, namely the extreme level of mortality caused by the Black Death and the remarkable similarity or consistency of the level of mortality, from Spain in southern Europe to England in northwestern Europe. The Black Death probably killed around 60% of Europe's population. It is generally assumed that population at the time was around 80 million. This implies that that around 50 million people died in the Black Death.

There are disputes still now about how many people died – whether it was 60% of the population of Europe or even more. The interesting question is, why did many never get the plague? Since today we don't know why many people do not get coronavirus, it's not surprising we can't answer that. What is clear is the Black Death changed society, accelerated the end of the feudal system and was a turning point, as well as a vast human tragedy; the Black Death of 1346–1353 is unparalleled in human history.

The next pandemic to consider is the 1665 Plague Year, which Daniel Defoe described in detail in *A Journal of the Plague Year*.

The first patient was probably George Viccars, a tailor's assistant in the village of Eyam in Derbyshire. In August 1665 he got a consignment of cloth from London. Within three weeks, he and his entire household were dead. Probably the cloth was infested with plague-carrying rat fleas. A first sign of infection was the sweet sickly scent of their own organs rotting internally. That helped persuade villagers that the disease could be transmitted through proximity.

One should never forget the human tragedy. One of the villagers in Eyam mourned his wife eloquently:

> This is the saddest news that ever my pen did write! The Destroying
> Angel, having taken up his quarters within my habitation, my dearest

Dear is gone to her eternal rest, and is invested with a crown of righteousness, having made a happy end. Indeed, had she loved herself as well as me, she had fled from the pit of destruction with her sweet babes, and might have prolonged her days, but that she was resolved to die a martyr to my interest. My drooping spirits are much refreshed with her joys, which I think are unutterable.

The ways Eyam responded to the plague have led to much research, because clearly some villagers had some sort of genetic protection, which scientists are still trying to analyse.

A Journal of the Plague Year

Daniel Defoe (1841) described the way many people 'went mad' as the plague skewered through London. Comets were the first omen of doom as

> two comets passed directly over the city, and that so very near the houses that it was plain they imported something peculiar to the city alone; that the comet before the pestilence was of a faint, dull, languid colour, and its motion very heavy, solemn, and slow; but that the comet before the fire was bright and sparkling, or, as others said, flaming, and its motion swift and furious; and that, accordingly, one foretold a heavy judgement, slow but severe, terrible and frightful, as was the plague; but the other foretold a stroke, sudden, swift, and fiery as the conflagration.

The conflagration was the Great Fire of London of 1666.

Defoe wrote that "the people, from what principle I cannot imagine, were more addicted to prophecies and astrological conjurations, dreams, and old wives' tales than ever they were before or since." He suspected some people made money out of these prophecies

> by printing predictions and prognostications – I know not; but certain it is, books frighted them terribly, such as Lilly's Almanack, Gadbury's Astrological Predictions, Poor Robin's Almanack, and the like; also several pretended religious books, one entitled, Come out of her, my People, lest you be Partaker of her Plagues.

Isaac Newton also lived through the plague, but the man who established the physical laws of the universe was of the opinion that the best way to cure it was to suspend a toad for three days in a chimney, mop up its vomit which would include bits of various insects, mash it all up and make it into lozenges. (*The Times* on 4 June 2020 covered the story with the headline "Newton's Plague Cure Fell Far From the Tree".)

Defoe had much compassion for those who became paranoid and con-fused: "One man wandered the streets crying, 'Yet forty days, and London shall be destroyed.'" Defoe was also dismayed by "the dreams of old women, or, I should say, the interpretation of old women upon other people's dreams; and these put abundance of people even out of their wits."

Some heard voices warning them the living would not be able to bury the dead. Others saw "hearses and coffins in the air carrying to be buried; and there again, heaps of dead bodies lying unburied, and the like, just as the imagination of the poor terrified people furnished them with matter to work upon." Ghosts were said to stalk the graveyards of the city and there often was a hubbub in Bishopsgate when a ghost appeared and disappeared as if called back to the underworld.

Defoe wrote:

> These things serve to show how far the people were really overcome with delusions; and as they had a notion of the approach of a visitation, all their predictions ran upon a most dreadful plague, which should lay the whole city, and even the kingdom, waste, and should destroy almost all the nation, both man and beast.

Defoe also attacked "those ministers that in their sermons rather sank than lifted up the hearts of their hearers". He pointed out that while the "whole Gospel is full of declarations from heaven of God's mercy, and His readiness to receive penitents and forgive them He allowed the people to suffer".

As in Defoe's time, conspiracy theories are also doing the rounds in the COVID-19 pandemic. A new study from the University of Oxford shows that people who hold coronavirus conspiracy beliefs are less likely to comply with social distancing guidelines or take up future vaccines. Research (Freeman et al., 2020) from a survey of 2,500 adults published in the journal *Psychological Medicine* in May 2020 showed that a disconcertingly high number of adults in England do not agree with the scientific and governmental consensus on the coronavirus pandemic:

- 60% of adults believe to some extent that the government is misleading the public about the cause of the virus
- 40% believe to some extent that the spread of the virus is a deliberate attempt by powerful people to gain control
- 20% believe to some extent that the virus is a hoax

These results matter, according to Freeman, Professor of Clinical Psychology, University of Oxford. Freeman et al. (2020) stated:

> Our study indicates that coronavirus conspiracy beliefs matter. Those who believe in conspiracy theories are less likely to follow government

guidance, for example, staying home, not meeting with people outside their household, or staying 2 metres apart from other people when outside. Those who believe in conspiracy theories also say that they are less likely to accept a vaccination, take a diagnostic test, or wear a facemask.

London recovered from the plague and the Great Fire, but between 1666 and 1918 there were many other plagues. One 20th-century pandemic was almost as deadly as the Black Death.

The Spanish flu (which did not start in Spain)

The 1918–1919 pandemic was caused by an influenza A virus known as H1N1. Epidemiologists still dispute the exact origins of the virus, but there is some consensus it was the result of a genetic mutation that perhaps took place in China. Despite being called the Spanish flu, the first recorded cases were in the United States. By March 1918 the country had been at war with Germany for 11 months. America's small, pre-war army had grown into a vast fighting force that would eventually send more than 2 million men to Europe (Spinney, 2018).

The men had to be trained before going to war. Fort Riley in Kansas was built to house some of the 50,000 new recruits. In early March a feverish soldier reported to the infirmary. Within a few hours more than a hundred other soldiers had come down with a similar condition, and more would fall ill over the following weeks. In April more American troops arrived in Europe and brought the virus with them. The first wave of the pandemic had arrived.

Spanish flu killed even more swiftly than the Black Death. There were stories of people waking up sick and dying on their way to work. Victims would develop a fever and become short of breath. Lack of oxygen meant their faces appeared tinged with blue. Haemorrhages filled the lungs with blood and caused catastrophic vomiting and nosebleeds. Victims drowned in their own bodily fluids. Unlike so many strains of influenza before it, Spanish flu attacked not only the very young and the very old, but also healthy adults between the ages of 20 and 40.

It has been calculated that the 13 weeks between September and December 1918 constituted the most intense period, taking the greatest number of lives. At least 195,000 Americans died in October alone. In comparison, total American military casualties for the whole of World War I came in at just over 116,000. Once again, it was the crowded military encampments where the second wave initially gained a hold. In September an outbreak of 6,674 cases was reported at Camp Devens, a military base in Massachusetts (Spinney, 2018).

Medical services began to be overwhelmed. Undertakers and gravediggers struggled, and conducting individual funerals became impossible. Many of the dead ended up in mass graves. The end of 1918 slowed the spread of the illness and January 1919 saw the beginning of the third and final phase. By then the disease was a much-diminished force. The ferocity of the autumn and winter of the previous year was not repeated, and mortality rates fell.

Lasting impact

The Spanish flu pandemic left almost no part of the world untouched. In Great Britain, 228,000 people died. The United States lost as many as 675,000 people, Japan some 400,000. The South Pacific island of Western Samoa (modern-day Samoa) lost one-fifth of its population. Researchers estimate that in India alone, fatalities totalled between 12 and 17 million. Exact data on the number of deaths is elusive, but global mortality figures are estimated to have been between 10% and 20% of those who were infected, according to Johns Hopkins University data, which is considered the most comprehensive database in the world.

In the COVID-19 pandemic, the most vulnerable now include those over 70, the obese and those with diabetes. These are understandable, but it is much harder to understand why black and minority ethnic men and women die more often. Many are doctors and nurses, so we should be careful before blaming it on poverty.

My final historical case study is fictional, based on the novel *La Peste*, written by Albert Camus (1947), a great novelist who died young, not of any illness but in a car crash.

In the middle of the Second World War Camus started to write *La Peste*. It is a fiction with lessons for us still. In March 1942, Camus told the writer André Malraux that he wanted to understand what plague meant for humanity: "Said like that it might sound strange", he added, "but this subject seems so natural to me" (Camus and Malraux, 2016). The two men never met but exchanged letters.

Eerie normality reigns in Oran in Algeria at first. Then, the horror begins. Dr Rieux (who Camus identified with) finds a dead rat. Soon the town is overrun with the mysterious deaths of thousands of rats. The rats are removed and the town heaves a sigh of relief, but Dr Rieux suspects that this is not the end. He has read enough about the structure of plagues and transmissions from animals to humans to be afraid.

"It's impossible it should be the plague, everyone knows it has vanished from the West," says one character. "Yes, everyone knew that", Camus adds sardonically, "except the dead."

For Camus, when it comes to dying, there is no progress in history, there is no escape from our frailty; being alive always was and will always remain a potential emergency, as one might put it, truly an inescapable 'underlying condition'. Camus's view is that our lives are fundamentally on the edge of what he termed 'the absurd'.

There is an interesting difference between attitudes to coronavirus and in Camus's novel. In Oran people are in denial. Even when a quarter of the city is dying, they keep imagining reasons why they will not get it. But there can never be safety – and that is why for Camus we need to love our fellow damned humans and work without hope or despair.

Camus (1947) wrote in *La Peste*:

> Pestilence is so common, there have been as many plagues in the world as there have been wars, yet plagues and wars always find people equally unprepared. When war breaks out people say: "It won't last, it's too stupid." And war is certainly too stupid, but that doesn't prevent it from lasting. The citizens of Oran were like the rest of the world, they were humanists: they did not believe in pestilence. A pestilence does not have human dimensions, so people tell themselves that it is unreal, that it is a bad dream which will end.

But Camus's hero Dr Rieux loathes this approach. The plague is not a punishment for anything deserved. That would be to imagine that the universe was moral or had some sort of design to it. But Dr Rieux watches a young innocent child die in his hospital and knows better: suffering is entirely randomly distributed, it makes no sense, it is no ethical force, it is simply absurd and that is the kindest thing one can say of it.

The doctor tries to lessen the suffering of those around him. But he is no saint. In one of the most central lines of the book, Camus writes: "This whole thing is not about heroism. It's about decency. It may seem a ridiculous idea, but the only way to fight the plague is with decency." A character asks Rieux what decency is. His response is as clipped as it is eloquent: "In general, I can't say, but in my case I know that it consists in doing my job."

Rieux's words, written over 75 years ago, sound exactly like the words many NHS doctors and nurses have said now.

Camus correctly sized up human nature and knew about a fundamental and absurd vulnerability in us that we cannot usually bear to remember. In the words of one of his characters, Camus knew, as we do not, that "everyone has inside it himself this plague, because no one in the world, no one, can ever be immune." That is precisely what we feel now. A Japanese publisher has just printed 150,000 copies of *La Peste*, so great is the demand as people look to it for insights.

Psychologists do not have particular qualifications for looking into the future, but it is hard to resist the temptation. The sunny-side-up school of psychology will point to greater awareness of the importance of communities and more willingness to help more vulnerable members of society. My question however, is will this last? Will we become better people? After the 1945 war Britain wanted change and enthusiastically voted in a Labour government. A nice clue to the decline of socialist ideals four years later is the wonderful 1949 comedy *Passport to Pimlico*. Thanks to an ancient charter, the borough of Pimlico finds it has the right to become independent, and does. It is bonanza time. It abolishes rationing and all restrictions over the border in the rest of Britain. Will our greater sense of being involved with each other last? It seems to me likely that for a while we will become more moral, more concerned, but then most of us will revert to type.

Some changes do seem likely. We will travel less for work and meetings will often be conducted by video conferencing. Those who see going away as an excuse for playing away may lament this, but it is environmentally very sensible. More people are likely to bicycle. If I were an inventor, I'd invent a tricycle for adults who can't manage to balance on two wheels.

The macro picture seems dire. The economies of the West will be hit hard and there will be higher unemployment, which will affect the mental health of thousands. Most of the world's stock markets have been stable or are even going up. Why is puzzling. More people will work from home. Is the result of more time together likely to be happiness for all? Co-op Legal Services (Telegraph Reporters, 2020) said in June in its newsletter that it had seen a 42% increase in divorce inquiries between 23 March and mid-May 2020, compared with the same period in 2019. The BBC's Today program on Radio 4 reported the same on 25 July. Sartre would not have been surprised.

We look to history to teach us, but remembering the lessons is not always easy.

Chapter 4

Variations in the national response to pandemics

Paths to success or failure

Mysteries and miseries of the virus

When 61 people met for a choir practice in a church in Mount Vernon, Washington, on 10 March, everything seemed normal. For two hours the choristers sang, snacked on cookies and oranges and sang some more. But one had been suffering for three days from what felt like a cold – and turned out to be COVID-19. In the following weeks, 53 choir members got sick, three were hospitalised and two died, according to a meticulous 12 May report by the US Centers for Disease Control and Prevention (CDC, 2020).

A database by Gwenan Knight and colleagues (Leclerc et al., 2020) at the London School of Hygiene and Tropical Medicine lists an outbreak in a dormitory for migrant workers in Singapore linked to almost 800 cases; 80 infections tied to live music venues in Osaka, Japan; and a cluster of 65 cases resulting from Zumba classes in South Korea. Clusters have also occurred aboard cruise ships and at nursing homes, meatpacking plants, ski resorts, churches, restaurants, hospitals and prisons. Sometimes a single person infects dozens of people, whereas other clusters unfold across several generations of spread in multiple venues.

"If you can predict what circumstances are giving rise to these events, the math shows you can really, very quickly curtail the ability of the disease to spread," say Jamie Lloyd-Smith et al. (2005) of the University of California, Los Angeles. But superspreading events are not well understood and not easy to study.

Some people infect many others and others don't spread the disease at all. In fact, the latter is the norm. Lloyd-Smith says: "The consistent pattern is that the most common number is zero. Most people do not transmit."

That's why in addition to R, scientists use a value called the dispersion factor (k), which describes how much a disease clusters. The lower k is, the more transmission comes from a small number of people. In a seminal 2005 *Nature* paper, Lloyd-Smith and co-authors estimated that SARS – in which superspreading played a major role – had a k of 0.16, "but we are certainly seeing a lot of concentrated clusters where a small proportion of people are responsible for a large proportion of infections." But Adam Kurcharski (2020) of the London School of Hygiene and Tropical Medicine estimated that k for COVID-19 is as low as 0.1. "Probably about 10% of cases lead to 80% of the spread," Kucharski says.

That could explain some puzzling aspects of this pandemic, including why the virus did not spread around the world sooner after it emerged in China. If k is really 0.1, then most chains of infection die out by themselves and SARS-CoV-2 needs to be introduced undetected into a new country at least four times to have an even chance of establishing itself. If the Chinese epidemic was a big fire that sent sparks flying around the world, most of the sparks simply fizzled out.

Why coronaviruses cluster so much more than other pathogens is an open question. Their mode of transmission may be one factor. SARS-CoV-2 appears to transmit mostly through droplets, but it does occasionally spread through finer aerosols that can stay suspended in the air, enabling one person to infect many.

Bake et al., in a 2019 study of healthy people, showed some breathe out many more particles than others when they talk. (The volume at which they spoke explained some of the variation.) Singing may release more virus than speaking, which could help explain the choir outbreaks. People's behaviour also plays a role. Having many social contacts or not washing your hands makes you more likely to pass on the virus.

Clearly there is a much higher risk in enclosed spaces than outside. On 22 April, *Nature* summarised the scientific research in China. Studying the spread of the coronavirus outside Hubei province – ground zero for the pandemic – *Nature* identified 318 clusters of three or more cases between 4 January and 11 February, only one of which originated outdoors. A study in Japan found that the risk of infection indoors is almost 19 times higher than outdoors, Derek Thompson (2020) reported in *The Atlantic* on 22 May 2020.

Some situations may be particularly risky. Meatpacking plants are likely vulnerable because many people work closely together in spaces where low temperature helps the virus survive. But it may also be relevant that they tend to be loud places, Knight says. The report about the choir in Washington made her realise that one thing links many clusters: they happened in places where people shout or sing. Knight added, as reported by Hamner et al. in 2020: "Maybe slow, gentle breathing is not a risk factor, but heavy, deep, or rapid breathing and shouting is."

Probably about 10% of cases lead to 80% of the spread, according to Kucharski. Timing also plays a role. Emerging evidence suggests COVID-19 patients are most infectious for a short period of time. Entering a high-risk setting in that period may touch off a superspreading event, Kucharski (2020) says: "Two days later, that person could behave in the same way and you wouldn't see the same outcome."

Countries that have beaten back the virus to low levels need to be especially vigilant for superspreading events, because they can easily undo hard-won gains. After South Korea relaxed social distancing rules in early May, a man who later tested positive for COVID-19 visited several clubs in Seoul; public health officials scrambled to identify thousands of potential contacts and rapidly found 170 new cases.

If public health workers knew where clusters are likely to happen, they could try to prevent them and avoid shutting down broad swaths of society, Kucharski (2020) says. "Shutdowns are an incredibly blunt tool," he says. "You're basically saying: We don't know enough about where transmission is happening to be able to target it, so we're just going to target all of it."

Korea learned the lessons of 2015

Television constantly plays old episodes of *M*A*S*H* with Alan Alda. The series is sympathetic to the Koreans but still portrays them as slightly provincial compared to the efficient American doctors. *M*A*S*H* remains a brilliant series, but its portrayal of Korea is outdated to say the least.

On 4 May 2015, a 68-year-old man in the horticultural business returned to Seoul after a business trip to Bahrain. A week later, he had a fever and was in pain. He visited several clinics before being admitted with what appeared to be pneumonia to Pyeongtaek St. Mary's Hospital. When his condition didn't improve, he was transferred to Samsung Medical Centre in Seoul. There he was finally diagnosed him with MERS or Middle Eastern respiratory syndrome on 20 May 2015. *The Lancet* (Cho et al., 2016) reported that by then he had spread the MERS coronavirus to 28 patients at the facilities.

One of those he infected became known as Patient 14 and he visited Samsung's emergency room on 27 May. Two days later when doctors learned that he might have been infected by the businessman who had been to Bahrain, Patient 14 was moved to an isolation room. It was too late; he had already infected 82 others. As a result, South Korea suffered the largest outbreak of MERS outside of the Middle East.

Korean officials made a number of mistakes in 2015. One was very understandable. The World Health Organization was providing information on MERS, but Bahrain didn't have any such cases and so the WHO did not mention the country. Therefore, South Korea paid no attention to the man returning from Bahrain.

There are also cultural differences in health care habits. In South Korea, hospitals often house four to six patients together per room. Rooms are always crowded with patients, health care workers and visiting families. You do not have to be a hypochondriac to visit several hospitals instead of going to a family doctor first. This journey around health facilities contributed to the explosion of MERS in South Korea.

Within 45 days, 186 patients were diagnosed and 38 died. With no sign of any vaccine, anxiety and fear caused by uncertainty became acute issues. In one study 1,656 people were not diagnosed with MERS but that did not stop them from worrying. About 7.6% had anxiety symptoms and more than about 16.6% were angry. Why were they being infected and affected?

After the outbreak, the Infectious Disease Control and Prevention Act, the legal framework for Korea's disease-prevention policy, was altered to allow disclosures. The South Korean government saw the importance of early warning and accurate diagnoses. Testing for MERS was cumbersome, and doctors had to wait several days to confirm a diagnosis. After the 2015 outbreak, South Korea enacted a new law that allowed laboratories to use unapproved in-vitro diagnostic kits in the case of a public health emergency.

As a result, South Korea responded well in 2020. As soon as news of the coronavirus outbreak in Wuhan became known, the South Korean government activated a 24/7 emergency response system to screen all travellers entering the country from Wuhan. And it quickly tracked the movement of infected people. Authorities watched closed-circuit television, investigated smartphone GPS data and publicised the histories of where COVID-19 patients moved. They were able to track and trace. Koreans could now learn where infected people went, when they were there and how they got there. If someone learned they might have been exposed, they could quickly visit a doctor and begin self-quarantine if they had symptoms.

The South Korean government soon tested an extraordinary number of people. By 26 February, the South Korean Health Department said it had tested 46,127 cases, while Japan had tested just 1,846 cases and the United States only 426. Between 20 January and 17 February, only 30 cases of COVID-19 were confirmed by the Korea Centers for Disease Control and Prevention. The country's disease prevention efforts were working effectively.

Then on 18 February a 31st case was reported in Daegu, the third-largest city in South Korea with some 2.5 million inhabitants. Patient 31 attended services at the Shincheonji Church of Jesus in Daegu. He ended up spreading the new coronavirus to 14 people in the congregation. Very quickly, COVID-19 cases in Daegu skyrocketed. By 29 February South Korea's Ministry of Health and Welfare reported 3,150 total confirmed cases, including 17 deaths. Many were the result of a religious mega-event held in Gwacheon city, Gyeonggi Province, on 16 February (Kupferschmidt, 2020).

The church seemed to have forgotten one of the Ten Commandments – thou shalt not bear false witness. It gave public health authorities a list of 1,290 members it said attended the event, but when an investigation team raided the church headquarters, it was soon clear that close to 10,000 members had actually gone to this event.

On 13 March, a new coronavirus case was reported in Seongnam, a city close to Seoul. The new case was connected to the River of Grace Community Church, which held services on 1 March and 8 March; 46 people who attended the services were infected. The continuing infections at religious events led to a bitter public debate on whether the Korean government could restrict religious activities in the case of emergency. Freedom of religion is guaranteed in the Korean constitution.

Pandemics often involve politics. South Korea's policies were utterly different to the approach that China employed. Beijing was dictatorial, even once it had decided the situation in Wuhan was so serious it could not be covered up. In Britain the satirical magazine *Private Eye* made fun of the confused political response. Unlike the South Koreans, the British government delayed putting track and trace into effect.

South Korea was not the only country to put effective measures into action. Germany moved quickly with an aggressive track-and-trace strategy that stalled the outbreak and prevented it from overwhelming the health system. On 27 February, the first confirmed case was reported in a local hospital in the Rhine-Neckar region. The victim had just returned from a skiing holiday in Italy.

The next day, the public health authority restructured all its departments towards crisis response. For example, staff who usually worked on dentistry or children's health were moved to public information call centres or processing testing data. And they were following a plan. The Robert Koch Institute, the German body in charge of the country's infectious disease response, had recommended widespread testing. The strategy was to test anyone who had symptoms and track down everyone they had contact with to isolate them as well. Doctors began a 'corona-taxi' service – checking up on asymptomatic people and keeping them away from hospitals. They built a separate facility to house COVID-19-positive care home residents, shielding other residents from them, while also keeping them out of intensive care units until necessary. None of this could have been done without widespread testing of suspected cases.

Germany and the UK logged their first coronavirus cases within two days of each other – 27 January in Rhine-Neckar and 29 January in York – but the two countries took very different paths. Germany did better on virtually all the measures while the UK has lagged behind – fewer tests, fewer hospital beds, tardier treatments – and the most telling measure of all, total deaths.

Symbols matter in any war – and this has been compared to a war with an invisible enemy. Boris Johnson did not wear a mask, nor did President Trump, who for weeks tried to minimise how lethal the virus was. As individual US states have much power under the Constitution, the president could not stop local governors being proactive. New York closed schools and businesses and initiated stay-at-home orders to stop the spread of coronavirus. It slowed the pandemic, but the New York governor, Andrew Cuomo, was frustrated that all these measures only slowed the spread of the virus. Other states that ordered lockdowns also saw slower than expected declines in coronavirus cases. Americans, it seems, have not been social distancing with any consistency and have been hampered by a haphazard federal response, struggles in testing, contact tracing and quarantining, and differences in how states responded. Deaths by

1 June in the United States totalled 106,195, making a mockery of the insouciance with which President Trump treated the virus. He repeated in his slurry of tweets that he did not think Americans would stand for staying home much longer and called shutdowns unsustainable.

That lack of a consistent, national message within the United States has created uncertainty. There are no travel restrictions within cities, within states or between states. The rules of lockdown vary by state and even sometimes by county, so individuals in lockdown areas are able to go across town lines to shops that are open.

"Signals are going out to the public all the time that we're essentially done with this," CNN's Chief Medical Correspondent Dr Sanjay Gupta (2020) said in May on CNN. "I think it's important to keep reminding people we need to stay vigilant on this."

By contrast, Greece, a country described in 2012 as bankrupt, managed to keep cases to a very low 175 deaths. The country found leadership in science through Dr Sotiris Tsiodras, an Athens-based pathologist and disease specialist, who quickly alerted politicians to the pandemic and was soon thereafter tasked with helping to oversee COVID-19 daily response briefings.

Greece's leaders were united in their response – and they acted on the scientific advice. The country also acted fast to begin cancelling large gatherings, including carnival celebrations on 20 February, after the country's third-identified coronavirus case. Strict and severe penalties including €150 fines for individuals who did not follow lockdown measures imposed on 23 March, culminating in about €4.25 million in fines collected. Greece's success is remarkable given its health budget had been slashed and that it was also dealing with thousands of migrants.

The psychology of uncertainty and the uncertainty of psychology

Norman Dixon's *On the Psychology of Military Incompetence* (1976) is a useful guide to why leaders make mistakes. Dixon showed how a fixed set of ideas and an inability to adapt to changing circumstances led to many military disasters. We may be seeing a repetition in the failure of some countries, including Britain, to deal with the virus.

Dixon stressed that in the 1939 war psychologists and psychiatrists were not allowed to participate in leader selection, because the military was sceptical about what they could contribute. Could you learn to command on the analytic couch? Never. Only the insistence of one the most enlightened men ever to occupy the post of the Adjutant-General of the British Army, General Sir Ronald Adam, overcame these obstacles. Between 1939 and 1945, Army psychiatrists, and subsequently psychologists, made valuable contributions to the question of training, officer selection, 'job satisfaction' and discipline. By the end of the Second World War, we knew a great deal about the nature of leadership on the level of pilots and platoon commanders. But no one so far had the temerity to apply the same criteria to the generals. Dixon did on paper years later, and caused a furor by showing how poor their decision making could be.

The failure of many countries, including Britain, to learn lessons from the handling of the virus is telling. Until the last week of May the professors on the SAGE committee, which advises the government on scientific issues, did not really explain that science could not provide definite answers as the data was so complex, while politicians sheltered behind the mantra that science was leading policy. Dixon's generals were often arrogant and inflexible too.

In mid-May 2020 the British finally decided to trial an app scheme on the Isle of Wight, which has 140,000 inhabitants. Some islanders objected, however, thinking this was a ploy to snoop on their lives. On 21 May it became clear that only a small fraction of the staff needed to track and trace the virus had been recruited, let alone trained. As of the beginning of June, less than 50% of the islanders have adopted the app and many of the trackers recruited complain that they have not been asked to track anyone at all (*The Times*, 1 June).

Bureaucracy usually loves secrecy. As it happens, I have been handed some correspondence dating back to 2006 from the Department of Health which shows how ancient and endemic the confusion about pandemics often is:

27 July 2006

Dear Colleague,

INFLUENZA PANDEMIC PLANNING OPERATIONAL GUIDANCE FOR SOCIAL CARE

Summary

I am writing to advise you of our plans to develop operational guidance for use by social care service commissioners and providers when planning for a possible influenza pandemic. We intend to publish this guidance for consultation by the end of September 2006. This letter also sets out actions councils and their partners could take in advance of the publication of the guidance.

Background

In England, we are accustomed to the annual round of influenza, which lays low a relatively small percentage of the population and is relatively mild in most cases. However, every few decades this annual occurrence reaches pandemic proportions.

You may be aware that, although the symptoms may seem to be similar, each year the influenza virus is slightly different. In fact the virus that causes influenza is constantly changing, or mutating, producing new strains. From time-to-time, a virus will develop which is sufficiently dis-similar to previous strains that the human immune system is caught out and takes longer than usual to adapt its defences in order to fight off the virus. As a result, the virus is able to infect more people than usual and spreads more quickly. For ease of reference I will refer to this type as influenza virus as 'pandemic flu'.

In the last century, there have been three outbreaks of pandemic flu, occurring in 1918, 1957 and 1968. Scientific evidence suggests that another pandemic is likely to occur in the near future, although it is impossible to predict exactly when that will be. However, the World Health Organization is on constant lookout for the first signs of pandemic flu emerging and will give the world as much advance notice as possible.

The impact of a flu pandemic on social services is likely to be intense and sustained. Advance planning will be key to ensure that social care organisations, their stakeholders and service users, are in the best possible position to manage such an emergency and lessen its impact.

We are developing operational guidance, specifically targeted at social care organisations and their partners and the issues relevant to contingency planning in social care. The guidance will be based on the actions set out in the UK Influenza Pandemic Contingency Plan and will complement other operational frameworks aimed at the NHS, schools and prisons and other sectors.

We intend to issue draft, but fit for purpose, guidance for consultation by the end of September 2006 with final guidance issued by December 2006, subject to consultation responses and agreement to a shortened consultation period.

An advisory group of key stakeholders will oversee and direct the development of the guidance.

Those stakeholders will include representatives from central Government, local authorities and the voluntary and private sectors. We will also explore how we can best involve frontline staff at this early stage.

Action to take now

As we do not know when the next pandemic will strike, it is important that Local Authorities and other social services organisations do not wait for the publication of guidance. It is important that you begin now taking positive steps to plan for the possibility of a pandemic.

In addition to the presence of Local Authority emergency planners on local resilience committees, it also very important that social services are well represented on contingency planning committees led by other public services, for example, Influenza Pandemic Planning Committees in each PCT.

Yours sincerely

Kathryn Hudson

Professor Lindsey Davies

Planning is excellent if it leads to action, but none of these recommendations were acted on. They would have cost money and, as Harold Macmillan observed, one of the pitfalls of politics is "events, dear boy". After the financial crisis of 2008, which led to austerity, planning for possible pandemics simply got put in a folder that might as well have been marked 'Do Something About It Sometime Maybe'.

By 2016, there was another flurry of concern about potential pandemics. The Scottish government organised a table-top exercise for how to handle a pandemic that highlighted anxieties about protective equipment for health staff, but no one seems to have shared the report much. In 2017, another report raised questions about preparations in the care home sector. In the middle of the pandemic, this sector became critical because people were moved to care homes from hospital sometimes without anyone knowing if they had the virus or could spread it.

Public Health England ran the new Cygnus exercise in October 2016, coordinating more than 950 people to test the UK's response to a new global pandemic. The exercise included four dummy meetings of Cobra, the government's emergency response system, over three days, as ministers and officials imagined the UK was trying to deal with influenza infections.

Asked about the report on Exercise Cygnus, the Health Secretary, Matt Hancock, said he had been assured by officials at the Department of Health that "everything that was recommended was done" (Pegg et al., 2020). However, Martin Green, the chief executive of Care England, which represents the largest independent care home providers, said concerns raised by Cygnus about the social care system's ability to handle a pandemic were never raised with the people who owned and ran the homes. If they had put in place a response, "we would have been in a much better place at the start of this pandemic," Green argued, as reported by Michael Day (2020).

Vic Rayner, the chief executive of the National Care Forum, was also critical: "The sort of plan you might anticipate coming from these recommendations has not been evident in terms of a national or local government approach. They might have done this planning behind the scenes, but they haven't involved the care providers" (Rayner, 2020).

"Nobody has ever had that conversation with us," she said. "Care England has been talking about providing extra capacity for years. We have been telling them that we have capacity and people don't need to be in hospital. But we have got nowhere."

Ironically, the government congratulated itself on preventing the NHS from being overwhelmed.

When the inevitable public inquiry happens, the psychological reasons for the British failure will have to be examined. I would recommend all members of the inquiry read Dixon's book on dithering generals as a start. One issue that will be central is that of excess deaths.

The calculation of excess deaths compares the number of deaths in a period with the number who have died in a similar period historically. On 30 June

2020, *MedicalXpress* claimed that since the virus hit, Britain was second only in excess deaths per million – 59,537 more deaths than usual since the week ending 20 March, indicating that the virus has directly or indirectly killed 891 people per million. At the time of writing, only Spain has 'scored' higher.

Another failing is that in the UK, both politicians and the civil service vacillated and were slow to react. As late as 9 March the government allowed the Cheltenham Festival to take place, where some 250,000 racegoers partied. The government also did not prevent Spanish supporters of Atletico Madrid from going to Liverpool for a football match, though the Spanish Club offered to refund fans who decided not to travel. The virus, if one may give the virus a line or two, said 'Hooray!'

One further British failure reflected ambivalence, it is safe to suggest. While a German test was available, the British government opted to develop its own in-house test, which came into use more than three weeks later. Meanwhile Britain stopped testing, saying it was not necessary. Then in late April the government announced that large-scale contact tracing and testing would be resumed. Winston Churchill is Boris Johnson's hero and Churchill sniped once that Captain Muddle was in charge of operations, they were inevitably bungled. That seems to have been the case in March and April 2020. The reasons were psychological and political. The ambivalence was perhaps because the UK did not want to depend on Germany. Power was concentrated and often hoarded in central bodies, especially Public Health England. Its chief executive got the virus and isolated himself, which may explain why he has hardly appeared to be questioned by the media.

The countries that have addressed the crisis well are dissimilar. Germany is not much like South Korea, and neither are like Singapore or Greece. What all three did was manage to concentrate on 'test and trace'. We do not know how many lives were saved as a result, but many probably were.

To complete this chapter on responses to the pandemic, it is worth mentioning the actor who played the ever-optimistic Forrest Gump. Tom Hanks and his wife, Rita Wilson, announced they contracted the virus while filming in Australia. Their calm response was reported in *Variety* on 20 April:

> Hello, folks. Rita and I are down here in Australia. We felt a bit tired, like we had colds, and some body aches. Rita had some chills that came and went. Slight fevers too. To play things right, as is needed in the world right now, we were tested for the coronavirus, and were found to be positive. Well, now. What to do next? The Medical Officials have protocols that must be followed. We Hanks' will be tested, observed, and isolated for as long as public health and safety requires. Not much more to it than a one-day-at-a-time approach, no? We'll keep the world posted and updated. Take care of yourselves! Hanx!
>
> (Stedman and Donnelly, 2020)

Chapter 5

Love in the time of plague
How social isolation can affect our relationships and sex life

If you are self-isolated you risk being bored, getting depressed and in some cases also becoming something of a hypochondriac, as one of my 35 correspondents has done. He is sleeping badly and frets his symptoms may or may not be the virus. Not all symptoms are as obvious as a fever and cough. A third symptom is loss of smell or taste. I will know I have the virus when I no longer enjoy my daily cigar and when I can't tell the difference between a decent brandy and mouthwash.

Self-discipline helps in this kind of crisis. So when you wake up, do not just wash your hands. Normal ablutions please – and clean your teeth especially. Dental surgeries have reopened, but a bad toothache is the last thing anyone needs now.

Then get dressed – and not as a slob. If you are alone, neglecting your appearance may not seem to matter since there is no one to see you, but it is often a sign of depression. So brush up. And look in the mirror. Check that you could go out looking like that.

If you are isolating with a partner, the problem is not to get ratty and snappy. Apart from holidays you probably have never seen so much of each other and now for most families there will be anxieties about work and money. It may seem absurd to turn to the rule of St Benedict for advice, but monks have known something since the earliest times. St Benedict's life in the 6th century had many dramas. Once while living in a cave above a lake as a hermit, the Devil showed him a beautiful, tempting woman. Did he succumb? No, he rolled his body into a thorn bush, which dampened his libido. Then some of the monks in the first monastery he set up tried to poison him because he was too demanding. But he did not let any of that stop him.

Much of St Benedict's rule is very Christian, but the most devout atheist should find nothing to bother them in the following pearls. Given they were celibates, it is curious how many of their rules seem wise for people who sleep together. And isolation is a testing time for that. Some of the relevant are:

> To do as one would be done by.
> To help in tribulation.

To console the sorrowing.
Not to carry anger into behaviour.
Not to prolong the duration of one's wrath.
Not to retain guile in one's heart.
To utter only truth from heart and mouth.
Not to return evil for evil.
Not to do injury, but to suffer it patiently.
To love enemies.

And though this is not part of the Benedictine rule, not to see those you live with as enemies.

In the monasteries, work was supposed to be shared equally. Again good advice, so any couple should be ready to change routines and make sure that chores are done equally. Swap who does the cooking, the gardening and the cleaning. Do not use the excuse that she or he is so much better at it than you are. Strangely enough anyone can learn to wash a basin, clean a toilet or make spaghetti Bolognese.

Psychologists like finding new therapies, so it shows how inventive we are that some psych has fangled up 'cleaning therapy'. To forget what is stressing you, don't lie down on the couch – clean it. The University of California gathered 30 couples for a study on stress hormones. Those who described their house as messy or chaotic had higher levels of cortisol, a steroid hormone produced in the adrenal gland in response to stress. Women were more adversely affected by clutter than men. Lucchessi (2019) reported this in the *New York Times* in an article summarising research on the point.

So, a messy home hurts your health. Decreasing the clutter would stop the build-up of cortisol and of stress. Also, cleaning offers more opportunities if you think psychologically. The Californians did not investigate what happened when couples cleaned together. Let us imagine A and B, who are managing to live together. It is just after dinner.

A: I'll do the dishes dear.
B: I'll hoover behind the sofa.

So far the A B dialogue is fine, if not exactly deep, but bite-my-tongue-out A is longing to snipe that B never bothers to clean behind the sofa, while B has denied himself the pleasure of putting the boot in the crockery by adding that when A does the dishes she leaves uneaten food and tomato ketchup smears.

Being together can expose the flaws in your relationship, which is why one rule is to think before you speak and not let long-simmering frustrations burst out. Self-discipline is important, especially because, if children are locked up with parents, seeing them upset it is likely to upset the children too. Avoid any spiral of spite with patience and good humour. If you feel like freaking out, give those around you some warning. Say you are going to freak out and if you are really in control, mime your insults and complaints, as suggested earlier.

Cleaning is not the only activity you can do together. If you are an older reader, the Royal School of Ballet runs an online program called Silver Swans. It offers ballet classes for seniors who have never danced before or for those who stopped when they were a child. The Duchess of Cornwall is a keen Swan, as is one of my 35 correspondents, who told me: "I haven't done anything like that since I was a teenager. It hurts but I feel after it, better than yoga."

One other Swan has posted on the Silver Swans website:

> As a child, I dreamed like a lot of little girls of being a ballet dancer and of course read the classic *Ballet Shoes* by Noel Streatfeild. I did not go to ballet classes as a child but thought what a wonderful opportunity it was to have a go as a 'silver' swan. So I went along and thoroughly enjoy the classes. It has been fun and challenging learning some basic ballet positions and trying to move gracefully to music.

Isolation is a chance to explore. So, get your dancing shoes out and also think what else you might like to delve into.

There is rather little evidence on how couples cope when they are forced together. However, at the University of Missouri-Kansas City, Leslie Stapley and Nancy Murdock (2020) studied how individuals can achieve a balance between togetherness and separateness in a way that helps them enjoy what they have. They concentrated on what they call the 'togetherness-separateness ratio'. Their conclusions were not surprising. The ability to maintain your sense of self independently of your relationship helps that relationship. It stops either partner feeling stifled. Stapley and Murdock (2020) collected data from 266 adults on self-differentiation (which is technical for maintaining your sense of self 'against' your nearest and dearest) time spent in leisure activities and shared leisure time satisfaction. The self-differentiation measure included questions designed to assess whether individuals preferred to maintain some emotional distance from others, were self-accepting, could make decisions on their own and felt emotionally stable.

Stapley and Murdock (2020) noted, "individuals who have higher levels of [sense of self] might be able to more effectively ask for desired time together and ask to do activities that are more personally meaningful, resulting in more enjoyable time together." In other words, if you know what you want to do in order to feel satisfied with a leisure time activity, you'll get more out of it, especially if your partner is willing to accommodate your desires. Those with a stronger sense of self-differentiation could tolerate much better situations in which they could not have their exact needs met.

Here, then, can be the key to maintaining separateness in the face of constrained togetherness. Within the confines of whatever space you are sharing, whatever its size, allow each of you to carve out room to get your own alone time. When you have little choice, finding your fulfilment as a couple may very well rest on maintaining your fulfilment as an individual.

Marriage, as Shaw observed, offers maximum opportunity. He had many issues about sex, which is why he added the downbeat phrase 'and the minimum of temptation'. For some couples, however, being together more than in normal life may actually make them more interested in sex.

This is a tread carefully issue, especially if your sex life has not been that good of late. In best guru mode I offer two ideas – one physical, one intellectual. The physical first. One warm-up idea is to try virtual swimming in your living room. No need to mention sex. You've never heard of virtual swimming? It is not hard. Lie down on the floor and make the same movements as in the crawl or breaststroke. There is no scientific evidence this has any effect, but it may make you laugh, which is never bad.

My second suggestion is to read poetry with your partner. A beautiful poem is a pleasure in itself and can be a good way into a subject. The English are supposed not to be passionate, but they have produced some of the greatest love poets – in the 17th century at least, with Andrew Marvell and John Donne, who was also Dean of St Paul's. For a priest, Donne was open in his eroticism, as this short extract shows:

> License my roving hands, and let them go
> Before, behind, between, above, below.
> O my America! my new-found-land,
> My kingdom, safeliest when with one man manned,
> My mine of precious stones, my empery,
> How blest am I in this discovering thee!
> To enter in these bonds is to be free;
> Then where my hand is set, my seal shall be.
> Full nakedness! All joys are due to thee.

If God had not wanted us to enjoy sex, Donne thought, He would have constructed us differently.

Some readers may notice that reading poetry and moving together as in virtual swimming may remind one of making love. This could be an opportunity to read some 'how to make love' books together. The market teems with them. I particularly like the title of *High Intensity Intercourse Training* and *Better Sex in No Time*. Does the title want to be taken literally? Does it mean it will tell you how to have an orgasm in 30 seconds or that reading this book will work in a trice? From personal experience I can recommend Alex Comfort's *The Joy of Sex*, which was a sensation when it first appeared in the 1970s. It is still selling solidly on Amazon.

As the time that *The Joy of Sex* was a best seller, a farce called *No Sex Please, We're British* was a huge West End hit. British tastes seem to have changed and isolation may help us explore our bodies and sensuality.

Chapter 6

Tensions during lockdown
Anger, irritation and emotional intelligence

"I wish you'd stop doing that."
"The more you drink the worse you get."
"Stop getting at me."
"You're so irritating."

These are typical snipes in domestic rows. Words can hurt but they do not usually maim. One of the dangers of the virus is that there is an increase in physical rows.

As China locked down, a 26-year-old woman named Lele found herself entangled in more and more arguments with her husband, with whom she now had to spend every hour in their home. On 1 March, while Lele was holding her 11-month-old daughter, her husband began to beat her with a highchair. She is not sure how many times he hit her. Eventually, she says, one of her legs lost all feeling; she collapsed on to the ground, still holding the baby in her arms.

A photograph she took after the incident shows the highchair lying on the floor in pieces, two of its metal legs snapped off – evidence of the force with which her husband hit her. Nearly every inch of her lower legs was covered in bruises, a huge haematoma blooming on her left calf.

Lele said that her husband had abused her throughout their six-year relationship, but that the COVID-19 outbreak made things far worse. Lele is not alone. The Metropolitan Police said they had made 4,093 arrests for domestic abuse offences – an average of about 100 a day – since 9 March, when people with coronavirus symptoms were asked to self-isolate (Snugs, 2020).

A British project called 'Counting Dead Women' has recorded at least 16 domestic abuse killings of women and children between 23 March, when the lockdown began, and 12 April. In Britain it is reckoned two women a day are killed by their partner.

In May 2020, the House of Commons Home Affairs Select Committee called for an emergency package of funding for support services for domestic abuse victims and vulnerable children. The Committee's chair, Yvette Cooper, said:

> Things are particularly hard for vulnerable children. We can't abandon them in the middle of this crisis. Local authorities, schools, the police

and other professionals involved in child welfare need to ensure they are working together to contact and visit homes where children are at risk.

Many countries have set up hotlines as governments try to address a crisis that experts say they should have seen earlier. "I urge all governments to put women's safety first as they respond to the pandemic," the Secretary General of the United Nations, António Guterres, wrote on Twitter.

The British government has invested £76 million additional funding for help for domestic abuse – and has tried to set up ways of alerting the police to incidents without the abuser, usually a man, knowing the police have been informed. This is timely. Marianne Hester (2020), a Bristol University sociologist, is one of many to argue that domestic violence goes up whenever families spend more time together.

Faced with the virus, and anxiety about the virus, we will need all our resources of both intelligence and emotional intelligence. People we love can exasperate us, not just because they are having a fling with the next door neighbour or have wasted money on what we might think is their idiotic hobby, but just by being themselves. Something they do grates; then everything they do grates. Normally you may be able to shrug it off, go for a walk round the block or just absorb it. Now, however, we are living in the new normal, which we would have once described as abnormal.

The more time you spend together, the more time for all those annoying habits to manifest themselves. Also, human beings sometimes give in to the 'imp of the perverse', as Edgar Allan Poe called it, so we sometimes do things that we know will irritate others we are close to.

A quick scan of the literature shows that one of the more ironic findings in psychology is that many relationships fracture during Christmas, which is not always a season of goodwill. Couples and families are forced to be together, and are expected to be happy and revel in good food and booze. Granddad insists the family play Cluedo while the children moan because they want to play Zombie Fingers, a game where you have to avoid being eaten alive by demented surgeons who love the gruesome. Everyone keeps glugging the beer, the chardonnay, the prosecco. Dad invents a new cocktail. The Romans had a saying – *in vino veritas*. The truth comes out when you drink.

At Christmas, we do not usually face risk from the outside. When we are forced into isolation by the virus, however, there is the plus that there is no pressure to be jolly, but there is a minus – an added dimension of anxiety. Is someone in the family about to start showing symptoms?

The hardest thing about isolation may be that spending so much time together under such worrying circumstances is not exactly romantic and does not make two people love each other more. Togetherness can infect doubts. It can make you wonder why you married or started to live with that person. An added burden is that economic anxieties caused by the virus are real. More people are in poverty – in America over 30 million have signed on for unemployment benefits and many of us are utterly unsure about our future.

Unlike anger, irritation has not been studied much by psychologists, yet there is evidence that what causes irritation can get out of control and lead to domestic violence.

It may be useful to offer an outline of how small disagreements can spiral into full-blown violence. That also suggests moments when one could change the situation. As with much else, this requires us to pay attention to how we feel and how those around us feel. It seems there are, as so often in psychology, stages.

Stages of irritation:

1   Being mildly annoyed or irritated.

One of the clichés of body language is that you start tapping your fingers as you get more annoyed.

2   Being seriously annoyed, which will usually involve saying how you feel.

It is always helpful to try to stop confrontations from getting out of hand. Taking the lead will mean one person saying firmly but without anger something like "Let's just pause a second and reflect on how we all feel." It may be optimistic to imagine that will work, but if you do not try, you will never know. So try, and try not to lose your cool if it fails.

The next three stages can be defined as follows:

3   Being angry.
4   Being so angry you threaten violence.
5   Violent incidents.

Police all over the world know that reports of domestic violence often lead nowhere. The Los Angeles Police Department (LAPD) has outlined some key features of domestic abuse and why such cases often lead to no criminal prosecution. Their list is complex, and it is usually obvious why isolation will often make the situation worse. The police summary is comprehensive:

> the victim loves the batterer . . . the batterer is not always violent.
> The victim fears the batterer, believing the batterer to be almost 'god-like.' Often threats are made against the victim, for example, the batterer will kill the victim if the beatings are reported to anyone. Police, in the victim's eyes, offer no long-term protection from the batterer.
> Fear: Often when the police come, the victim will not admit she – and it is most often the woman – she suffered any battering.
> The victim may be economically dependent on the batterer.

People feel they must stay in a relationship and are highly resistant to change as a means of problem solving.

> Socialization and/or religious or cultural beliefs demand that the victim maintain the facade of a good marriage.
>
> Often the batterer is the victim's only psychological support, having systematically destroyed the victim's other friendships. Other people also feel uncomfortable around violence and withdraw from it.

The summary also refers to learned helplessness. I described a series of studies by Seligman earlier. The Los Angeles Police adopted this idea and argued that victims had been taught to be powerless, and therefore did not think that they could change the situation.

> Often the victim stays for the sake of the children 'needing a father,' or the batterer may threaten the children if the victim tries to leave. The batterer frequently threatens to take the children away from the victim if the victim leaves, and the victim believes the batterer.
>
> The victim believes police may not take domestic violence seriously, hence the victim believes the batterer is often not punished or removed from the victim. Yet any attempts by the victim to consult authorities are seen as a threat by the batterer and he/she may beat the victim for that.
>
> Sometimes the batterer is otherwise well respected or mild mannered, so the victim's concerns are not taken seriously. Often the batterer is violent only with the victim and frequently concludes there is something wrong with the victim.
>
> The victim may rationalize the beatings, believing that the victim must have 'deserved' the 'punishment' or that the batterer was just 'too drunk' to know what the batterer was doing (beliefs the batterer propagates).
>
> The victim may have no idea that services are available and may feel trapped.
>
> The battering takes place during a relatively short period of time. Afterwards the batterer may be quite gentle, apologetic, loving, and may promise never to beat the victim again.
>
> Often a battered person, motivated by pity and compassion, is convinced that the victim alone can help the batterer with the 'problem' (whether it is drinking, 'pressure from the outside world,' 'victim's mistakes,' etc.).

The LAPD summary does not mention alcohol or drugs, but the evidence shows that in isolation some people drink more, sometimes much more. The World Health Organization (2004) estimates 55% of domestic abuse incidents involve alcohol.

A May 2020 survey by You Gov Polls shows people in the UK are drinking differently as a result of coronavirus. More than one in three of the 1,555 drinkers surveyed said that they have either stopped drinking or reduced how often they drink since the lockdown. Six percent have stopped drinking entirely.

However, some people are drinking more: 21% admitted that they have been drinking more frequently since the lockdown. This suggests that around 8.6 million UK adults have increased their alcohol consumption under lockdown. Some aspects of lockdown encourage drinking. Parents have suddenly found themselves having to home school and entertain children all day. A simple pleasure at the end of another frantic day may be entirely deserved in the eyes of many. Research shows alcohol makes us feel 'happier' in the moment (Geiger and MacKerron, 2016), energised, relaxed, sexy and confident (Ashton et al., 2017).

One in 14 survey respondents felt that alcohol had made the tension in their household worse since lockdown. If we apply this to the UK adult population, we can infer that more than 3.5 million adults are living in households where alcohol has exacerbated tensions. The figures are even higher for households with children. One in seven people with children under 18 living in their household reported that alcohol had increased tensions, while only 4% felt alcohol had lessened tensions.

The lockdown is also likely to change the way some casual users of cannabis or cocaine use drugs. Launching a 2020 survey, Professor Adam Winstock, the founder and director of the Global Drug Survey, warned some drug users could also switch to harder drugs, increasing the risk of dependency and overdose (Winstock et al., 2020). Supplies of some prescription drugs could start to run out in the coming weeks, he added, leading users to take more dangerous alternatives. Some homeless users in the UK were turning to heroin and alcohol because of a shortage of synthetic cannabinoids, such as spice.

Gail Gilchrist et al. (2019), of the National Addiction Centre at King's College London, argued these trends were likely to lead to a greater risk of addicts abusing their partners when they were in withdrawal or craving alcohol and heroin.

The irritation data

Sometimes when you start to study a subject, you do not know where that will lead. In 2019 I began a study of irritation, not imagining the early findings would be relevant now, as lockdowns put us together more than usual. There have been many studies of anger, which is more extreme than irritation, as it is often accompanied by distressed behaviour. We clench our jaws or grind our teeth. We also get stomach aches, experience increased and rapid heart rate, get sweaty palms, feel hot in the neck/face and, if very angry, start shaking.

Irritation does not produce such dramatic effects, which may be why there are only six entries on the subject in the British Library catalogue. I asked people to keep diaries of what irritated them and got interesting data, which ranged from the predictable to the surprising. Some individuals have a gift for being irritating, like Japan's Olympics Minister, Yoshitaka Sakurada. The *Bangkok Post* reported on 14 January 2016 that he came under fire for describing so-called comfort women, who had been forced to have sex with Japanese war-time troops, as 'professional prostitutes'. He ignored the fact that if they did not oblige, the women were likely to be killed. In 2018, he was appointed Minister for Computer Affairs and soon admitted he did not touch a mouse or keypad. Why should he bother? Minions could do that for him.

Finally, Sakurada annoyed fellow politicians because he turned up three minutes late for a parliamentary meeting. Opposition MPs said being so late – three minutes! – showed disrespect for his office; they boycotted a meeting of the budget committee for five hours in protest. *Asahi Shimbun* (2019), one of the most respected newspapers in Japan, asked readers if Sakurada should keep his job; only 13% backed him.

Bearing him in mind, consider the list of irritants below, which stem from my research. It is very human in its variety. Forty-two people kept diaries and sent them to me. The notes they provide are of events that can happen in isolation.

> *Guys who pee on the toilet seat and don't clean it up.*
> *Noisy neighbours.*
> *Snagging a fingernail, having to untangle said fingernail from new jumper.*
> *People tapping their fingers to music for extended periods of time.*
> *People who have their headphones up too loud.*
> *Really loud children, and the parents who refuse to keep them in line.*

>> *Lights left on.*
>> *Inefficient/slow service.*
>> *Inefficient processes/processing.*
>> *Lack of napkins.*
>> *Cutlery that is too big.*
>> *Having the way I put a nappy on changed as it 'wasn't straight' and other such similar situations.*
>> *People who cannot follow simple instructions.*

> *Elasticated jeans falling down at the waist and having to be pulled up.*
> *Loud sudden noises from building sites or passing motor bikes breaking the peace and not allowing conversation.*
> *People making a telephone call and not giving their name – assuming I know who they are and then starting to talk without checking I have time to finish the discussion.*

*Mansplaining – usually men, but not necessarily, who launch into a conde-
  scending explanation of something I usually know far more about than
  them. It's either because I'm a woman or because I'm older.*
*Myself for getting things wrong – catching the wrong train, losing my bank
  card, forgetting my keys.*
Curtains not drawing fully and letting a slice of light through.
People scuffing their shoes as they walk along the pavements.
Not being able to recall a name on the tip of my tongue.
Smell of the food of barbecues next door.
*The automated message – 'the number you are calling knows you are waiting'
  repetition.*
Sniffing continuously.
Burnt saucepans.
Leaky shoes.
Shoelaces that fray and are too short.
Shoes that need fixing.
People who don't apologise when they've done something wrong.
Little lights that shine in the night.
Things getting in the way of your view.
Not being able to see round corners.
*Noises, followed by health issues, getting stuck in traffic, computer and mobile
  phone malfunctions.*

Six kinds of irritation were personal:

Being irritated by oneself.
Work conflicts and disappointments.
Partners causing irritation.
Children, almost invariably one's own.
Being made to wait.
Being owed or owing money.

And, very relevant in this crisis:

Politicians.

Usually we discuss irritations irritably. But it can be turned into a game.
Being playful may help, as there will be some families who do not find it easy
to approach any of this without tensions.

Sit comfortably and, keeping it as light as possible, ask everyone in your
  household:
What do I do that irritates you?
Once they have said, ask then to score your irritation out of 10.

You now will have an irritation score for everyone in the house.
And someone will be awarded the prize for being the Top Irritant.

Then suggest what you might do to change the irritating behaviour. For example, if you promise not to X, I will promise not to Y. Mrs Thatcher once said that the family was the one institution where bargaining did not take place; it was an unusually romantic view for her. In discussing some ideas for defusing tensions, it's clear they do often involve bargaining. I suggest:

> Talk more to each other so that you can identify all the mannerisms and other things that irritate all the people in the family.
> Touch more when it comes to people in your own household and wives, husbands, partners. I'm not talking sex here, but affection. Touch is reassuring.

Some people will find erotic possibilities in the isolation, as discussed in Chapter 5.

Emotional intelligence

Discussing what irritates you is also a good introduction to the subject of emotional intelligence, which is very different from what we usually understand as intelligence in the IQ test. The history of IQ goes back to the mid-1890s in Paris. The city authorities commissioned two psychologists, Binet and Simon, to assess how clever schoolchildren were and to help find ways of helping those who lagged behind. The tests had questions like:

> If Andrew eats six grapes and two apples, how many pieces of fruit has he eaten?

The answer is eight; there is no leeway. Binet and Simon's work became the basis for the intelligence test and IQ. There have been hundreds of studies of how accurate and useful IQ tests are and whether they discriminate against certain groups. It was only in 1985, however, that psychologists began to wonder if there might not be an entirely different kind of intelligence. Emotional intelligence was only 'discovered' in 1985 when Leon Payne submitted a PhD thesis called *A Study of Emotion: Developing Emotional Intelligence*. It became famous when Daniel Goleman (1995) discovered an article on academic research that followed on Payne. The 'discovery' made was that some people were better than others at identifying their own feelings, identifying the feelings of others and solving problems involving emotional issues.

Goleman had been planning a book on what he then called 'emotional literacy' but he thought 'emotional intelligence' would make a better title. The book stayed on the *New York Times* best-seller list for a year. It made such an impact partly because he claimed emotional intelligence was the largest single predictor of success in the workplace. Emotional intelligence requires "the ability to process emotional information, particularly as it involves the perception, assimilation, understanding, and management of emotion", Goleman (1995) said.

Psychologists have analysed emotional intelligence in four components. The first is emotional identification, perception and expression, which involves such abilities as identifying emotions in faces, music and stories. Strong emotional intelligence allows one to manage feelings about oneself and others, and to appreciate the perspectives of other people and how they feel or think about things.

Emotional intelligence is helpful in lockdown partly because it helps you to pause and think before you react. Learning to listen and learning not to respond defensively when you are criticised is showing emotional intelligence. This is a difficult area because you may think you do listen and are not defensive, while others do not see you like that. There is no quick fix, but you could steel yourself to be tolerant and to consider their point of view. Honour differences, as it were.

Developmental psychologists have done much work on when children start to realise that other people think and feel differently. The great child psychologist Jean Piaget claimed children were egocentric until they were five or six. They could not imagine how a scene looked from someone else's point of view. Many experiments – most notably by Hughes (1978) and Bryant (1982) – proved this was wrong. Children could imagine how a scene looked from different angles, so they were not wholly egocentric.

Seeing different points of view may be hard if you are more with your family than ever before. If one of your children is upset, don't get angry or upset, but try turning it into a game where you see who remembers conversations better. Fun is needed in isolation.

Chapter 7

The impact of lockdown on children

Attachment, mental health and resilience

There is evidence that the embryo can feel from 20 weeks after conception. Imagine how the embryo feels as the moment of birth nears, 16 or so weeks later. She or he has spent nine months inside, inseparable from the mother. Then she or he struggles down the birth canal into the world and becomes a separate human being who is utterly helpless and dependent. Usually as soon as the baby is born, he or she is given to the mother to hold. And babies need to be held.

In 2018 I filmed in an Israeli hospital that often took in Syrian patients who had been injured in the civil war being fought across the border between forces loyal to the dictator Al Assad and rebels. In the children's ward a little girl – no one knew her real name or age but at most she was 18 months old – was crying.

She wants her mother, said the doctor, and added that babies, whether they are Jewish, Arab, Chinese or anything else, all want their mother to hold them.

A nurse picked the child up and cuddled her, which calmed her a little.

I asked what would happen to her.

The doctor said they would arrange for her to go back to Syria. In 2018 many Syrians were allowed into Israel to get medical treatment and then returned to Syria. All the hospital could do for now was feed her, clean her and give her that essential cuddle.

Touch reassures because it tells you someone cares. Studies at the Mayo Clinic suggest that premature babies who are stroked often grow 40% faster than those who are not. May (2018) also found that cancer patients who were touched got improved autoimmune responses.

If no one touches you – and this has nothing to do with sex – you are likely to feel no one cares. One of the tragedies of coronavirus is that it has made it possible, even prudent, to put barriers between a sick person and their family.

Hospitals and care homes in Europe are now regularly having to deny members of families the chance to be with their relatives in the last few hours of their lives. They could infect others, so coronavirus defeats compassion. If you can only look at your father through a screen, something crucially human is lost.

The largest experiment on the effects of separation took place during the Second World War. In 1939 the government put a plan to evacuate children into action. Evacuation day was a deeply emotional and often traumatic experience for all involved and full of uncertainty and tearful goodbyes. Although some children were excited at the prospect of the forthcoming 'adventure', most evacuees were unaware of where they were going, what they would be doing and when they would be coming back. Faced with enormous upheaval and prolonged separation from loved ones, the initial separation was devastating and heart-rending for both mothers and children as whole families were dislocated and uprooted. However, the fear of bombing attacks meant that most parents considered evacuation for the best, as children would be safer away from the city. Yet, evacuation was not compulsory, and some parents were understandably reluctant to take part, despite propaganda posters that encouraged co-operation. For those parents who did co-operate, it would be a nervous wait of several days to find out where their children had gone, with notification coming via a postcard through the mail.

At the start of the war, Freud was in London with his wife, his daughter Anna and Anna's partner, Dorothy Burlingham. Anna was a well-respected child psychoanalyst and the two women set up the Hampstead War Nurseries for children. Freud and Burlingham found that being separated from their mothers was even more stressful for the children than the air raids. Many of the children had spent some time in an underground station which housed 5,000 people. The nursery was very comfortable after that.

The work in the Hampstead nursery influenced attachment theory, which showed how babies need presence and holding. If a mother, father or carer does not respond to their baby's signals, it becomes distressed and eventually withdrawn.

In 1971 I interviewed John Bowlby, the doctor and psychoanalyst who developed attachment theory, which is described here. Bowlby became one of the most influential voices of the post-war era in this field. He told me (Cohen, 1971),

> If you put an infant of between nine months and three years in a strange place with strange people he is very frightened and upset. He cries for long periods and makes it obvious he wants to find his mother. This is the stage of protest. Then he begins to despair. He can become very apathetic, very distant. He may cease crying or even talking. When the child has been separated for 14 or 21 days he tends to evade her. Sometimes he tends not to recognise her. All the normal emotional reactions are missing.

Bowlby emphasised mothers. His son Sir Richard Bowlby told me in an interview (2018) that his father began to realise that fathers also played a central role – and much evidence shows fathers are much more involved now in looking after children. Marcoux (2018) summarised the changes. Back in 1982, 43% of fathers admitted they had never changed a diaper. Today, that number is down to about 3%, and the consequences are far-reaching. When dads dress, diaper and bathe their babies, the father-child relationship grows stronger as the child grows.

Research shows that young fathers today have more egalitarian beliefs about child care and are striving to see more even distribution of parenting duties in their own households. The numbers prove things are not perfect – many fathers admit they still do less than their partners, but they are spending more time with their children than previous generations.

There is now neurological support for attachment theory, though it is still focused on mothers. Mothers' and babies' brains can work together as a 'mega-network' by synchronising brain waves when they interact. When mothers express more positive emotions, their brain becomes much more strongly connected with their baby's brain.

The research (Leong et al., 2020), published in the journal *NeuroImage*, used a method called dual electroencephalography (EEG). Electrodes are placed on the scalp to follow electrical signals in the brains of two people, in this case the brain activity of mothers and babies while they are interacting with each other. They tended to synchronise their brain waves – an effect known as interpersonal neural connectivity. As a result, the mother's and the baby's brains operated together as a network, a fusion helped by much eye contact between the two.

"From our previous work, we know that when the neural connection between mothers and babies is strong, babies are more receptive and ready to learn from their mothers," said Dr Vicky Leong in the University of Cambridge's Department of Psychology, who led the study.

> At this stage of life, the baby brain has the ability to change significantly, and these changes are driven by the baby's experiences. By using a positive emotional tone during social interactions, parents can connect better with their infants, and stimulate development of their baby's mental capacity.

"Our emotions literally change the way that our brains share information with others – positive emotions help us to communicate in a much more efficient way," said Dr Leong and added:

> Depression can have a powerfully negative effect on a parent's ability to establish connections with their baby. All the social cues that normally foster connection are less readily available to the child, so the child doesn't receive the optimal emotional input it needs to thrive.

Emotional communication between parents and children is crucial during early life, yet little is known about its neural underpinnings. This is the first brain imaging study of two related individuals to investigate if and how babies' interpersonal neural connectivity with their mothers is affected by the emotional quality of their social interaction. When the baby does not get that connectivity, it despairs, as Bowlby pointed out. It feels abandoned.

How to help children deal with the pandemic

The virus hit at a time when there has been more discussion of child mental health than ever before in the developed world. Events such as 9/11, Hurricane Katrina and the 2008 earthquake in Sichuan, China, have already helped mental health researchers see how young people typically react during a crisis. Now, two studies – one in Toronto and another in Baltimore – will monitor the emotions and behaviours of children and teens through this pandemic. What they reveal may teach parents and other adults how to help children in later waves of the coronavirus – or during the next major crisis.

Social media and the internet brims with advice – good, bad and ridiculous. Here is an example, and readers may decide into which of the three categories it fits. "If your child is under 6 and has not heard about the virus yet, you may not want to bring it up, as it may introduce unnecessary anxiety," said Abi Gewirtz (2020), PhD, a clinical psychologist and professor at the University of Minnesota, and the author of the forthcoming book *When the World Feels Like a Scary Place: Essential Conversations for Anxious Parents and Worried Kids*.

Unless you are living in a cell with no contact with the outside world, it's unlikely your children will not have heard of the virus. It's also to be hoped they are not told to think of it like this: "There's lots of icky bugs going around and we're going to hang tight at home so they can clean the schools out."

No wonder President Trump may have thought bleach was a way of wiping out COVID. Bleach does kill icky bugs.

The past does offer some clues to ways of helping, and for many children the visual helps. The Austrian artist Friedl Dicker-Brandeis helped distract children brought to the Nazi's Theresienstadt concentration camp in Czechoslovakia with clandestine art lessons that have since been considered an early form of art therapy. Drawings by young students who survived the nuclear attack on Hiroshima were presented in the 2013 documentary *Pictures From a Hiroshima Schoolyard*. Pictures created by Syrian children in UNICEF-supported schools are both hopeful and haunting.

"If you think about children as meaning makers, they're constantly trying to make meaning of this," said University of California, San Francisco psychologists Chandra Ghosh Ippen and Alicia Lieberman (2019), who argue that children try to make sense of how much danger they and their family are in.

The UN Secretary-General Antonio Guterres (2020) has warned that the coronavirus pandemic is putting many of the world's children "in jeopardy" and urged families everywhere and leaders at all levels to "protect our children" whose lives "are being totally upended" by the virus. He added the global recession could lead to "hundreds of thousands of additional child deaths in 2020. This would effectively reverse the last two to three years of progress in reducing infant mortality within a single year." This estimate was based on a 2011 paper by three economists – Sarah Baird, Jed Friedman and Norbert Schady – who investigated the impact of 'income shocks' such as a recession on infant mortality.

In an overview on 10 May the World Health Organization (2020) said 188 countries have imposed countrywide school closures, affecting more than 1.5 billion children and young people. And it said nearly 369 million children in 143 countries who rely on school meals for daily nutrition must now look to other sources. Guterres said some schools are offering online learning, but children without access to the internet and in countries with slow and expensive services are severely disadvantaged.

Naomi Fisher (2020) has written on the psychological effects of teaching children at home. She quotes the developmental psychologist Alison Gopnik, who stresses that social learning at home can be richer and more meaningful than school learning. Fisher warns that what works at school may not work at home. At school, the whole system is set up to ensure children comply. At home, children have more power. They can say no more easily, and they do. It may be wiser in the long term to focus on finding things the child is interested in and learn about that, rather than fighting about worksheets.

Fisher (2020) provides a nice image: "Trying to persuade a bored child to learn is like trying to fill a sieve with water. Even when it appears that they are learning, nothing sticks. Look for their interest and follow that." In trying to teach your child, Fisher advises you to think about what control you can give them in increase their sense of autonomy. "For older children, this may mean keeping out of the work sent to them by school and leaving it up to them what they do – and when." She adds:

> We're in the middle of the most anxiety-provoking time globally our children (and us!) have ever experienced. Many children are hyper-aroused, and they show this with anger and resistance. If parents react with anger, then the child becomes even more anxious and more resistant.

Her advice is that parents need to stay calm, even whilst their children shout and rage. This is an extraordinary time. She continues:

> Our children will remember this time forever. Perhaps the most important thing they are learning is how we deal with a crisis and what our priorities are. Protecting their wellbeing and our relationship with them will mean that they can learn more efficiently both now and in the future.

One of the basics parents must do is to tell their children the rules of good hygiene. Parents must make sure children are washing their hands for at least 20 seconds before and after meals, after they go to the bathroom, after they come in from outside and after they've blown their nose or put their hands in their mouth.

Several experts sensibly recommend making hand washing into a game. "You can even make it into a competition," said Judith Matloff (2020), who teaches conflict reporting at Columbia University Graduate School of Journalism and is the author of the upcoming book *How to Drag a Body and Other Safety Tips You Hope to Never Need: Survival Tricks for Hacking, Hurricanes and Hazards Life Might Throw at You.* Matloff suggests you compete with your children to see who can wash their hands the longest, or who can make the suds the biggest.

For most families, the main problems are easy to define but not necessarily easy to solve. Not knowing is likely to make children anxious, so explain to your children what is going on. Obviously it is virtually impossible to do that with children who are three or younger, but even 3-year-olds usually understand the word 'ill'. One way is to say that there are thousands of people who are ill and you have to be very careful not to get ill yourself. With young children, pictures can help.

Professor Robin S. Cox of Royal Roads University in Victoria, Canada, leads the Resilience by Design Research Innovation Lab. She argues drawing can help children express emotions they may not even know they have. "Children may not have as much access to physical activity, which is another way of managing anxiety and fear," Cox (2020) said. "So [art] provides another way of managing anxiety and engaging with those emotions."

Ghosh Ippen is the associate director of the child trauma research program at the University of California, San Francisco, and has written several illustrated books for children on coping with trauma. "In drawings, you can do things that in life you can't do," she said and added.

> You can have the coronavirus be a thing. When you personify something, when you give something a body, you're able to talk about it, you're able to manage it. In play, kids are able to beat it up, they're able to jail it, they're able to yell at it, they're able to say, "Hey, you go away!"
>
> (quoted in Ipeen and Leiberman, 2019)

Sociologists Alice Fothergill and Lori Peek (2015) spent seven years studying children who were directly affected by Hurricane Katrina, which displaced more than a million people from the Gulf Coast in 2005. In *Children of Katrina* (Fothergill and Peek, 2015), they explored how children, aged 3 to 18 at the time of the storm, fared in the disaster. They described three post-disaster trajectories – declining, finding equilibrium and fluctuating – and explored the social forces and factors that influenced children's recovery.

"The kids were all drawing these pictures that always had black or brown crayons to colour this dark, murky water," said Peek, professor of sociology at the University of Colorado, Boulder (Fothergill and Peek, 2015). And added:

> And sometimes it was kids who'd been in the water, who'd really seen the water. Sometimes it was kids who hadn't seen it, but they knew about it through the media, or just through stories. But there was this remarkable consistency in what children were colouring.

Peek believes that children's responses to the current pandemic will be like responses to past 'slow-motion' disasters:

> I think some of the creative interventions that children may be drawing in the context of climate change, or in the context of Katrina – where the emergency period lasted for a long period of time – might have certain parallels to what you're seeing with COVID.

Make the virus personal

Children like to draw and paint, so get them to draw a picture of the family, then of the outside world, then of the virus, which is attacking both. By giving the virus a shape they create, children get some control, so it does not seem so powerful. Here are some ideas to get you going:

> Vampire
> Dragon
> Creepy crawley
> Robot

Keeping track of the moods of children is necessary and especially getting a sense of when they are angry or confused, because the whole situation is so different from their normal lives. The study of child development has been a boom area in psychology in the last 20 years. Inevitably, psychologists have even developed an anger inventory for children aged from 7 to 17 (Steele et al., 2009).

Some of the questions or statements on which children are asked to rate themselves follow. Normally psychologists would just ask the questions, but you could try miming when asking them. I do not mean to be patronising, but I offer some suggestions about what one may mime. Turning serious questions or statements into a role-play exercise can defuse the stress. The statements that follow give everyone some chance to exaggerate and let off some steam.

> "I feel angry."
> Huff and puff and say you're furious.

More tricky is the statement "I feel like breaking things."
Pick up a plate and pretend to throw it, looking furious. You are likely
to feel better.
"I feel like yelling at someone."
So yell very loud.
"I get very impatient if I have to wait for something."

This is less easy to act out. One way is to say you are waiting for someone to
turn up – and they are late. First 5 minutes, then 15 minutes, then 30 minutes
late. Imagine how you would respond at each time interval. And then what
you would do when they finally appear.

"I feel grouchy or irritable."
Get the children to do a very expressive grouch.
Other statements are:
"I get in a bad mood when things don't go my way."
"I get very angry if my parent or teacher criticises me."
"I get in a bad mood easily."

A second part of the inventory looks at how children express their frustrations. Do not let academics rule your choices; find out whether other statements might be more relevant for your child and ask children to add what
feels right for them. Again, miming is a good device and gives the chance to
act out being impatient, bad tempered and sulky, which can be entertaining
and can defuse some pent up feelings.

"I slam doors or stomp my feet."
"I argue or fight back."
"I hit things or people."

Teenagers

Teenagers will be able to understand the basic issues around the virus, but
they may well feel trapped and want to escape the confines of a now very
confined family life. Again, the only answers are to say to them they can say
whatever they like. Feelings are better out than in. Do not get angry with
them for expressing their frustration. Easy to say, but harder to do. Teenagers
may well worry about falling behind in school and missing exams, so be ready
to ask their school when they will be going back and what the provisions for
exams are.

In Britain the mental health charity Young Minds (2020) surveyed 2,111
young people aged 13 to 25 who said they had a history of mental health
needs. The survey was carried out between Friday 20 March 2020, the day on
which schools closed to most students, and Wednesday 25 March.

Eighty-three percent of respondents agreed that the coronavirus pandemic had made their mental health worse while 32% said it had made their mental health 'much worse'; 51% said it had made their mental health 'a bit worse'. It was worrying that 26% of young people who had been accessing support said that they were not currently able to get any.

When asked to share how different activities affected their mental health, respondents reported that face-to-face calls with friends (72%), watching TV/films (72%), exercise (60%) and learning new skills (59%) were helpful, while 66% of respondents agreed that watching or reading the news was unhelpful.

The charity also asked about the factors that affected young people's mental health and what they were most worried about. Common answers included concerns about their family's health, school and university closures, loss of routines and coping mechanisms, isolation and a loss of social connections.

Emma Thomas (Young Minds Charity Report, 2020), Chief Executive of Young Minds, said:

> We also know that many young people who previously might not have needed mental health support are likely to do so in future. As the impact of the pandemic and the restrictions on their lives continues to sink in, more young people are likely to struggle.

The charity published two responses by its activists as being typical. Twenty-two-year-old Jacob said:

> My panic attacks have come back for the first time in three years and I've found it difficult to sleep and eat well. My counsellor is continuing my weekly sessions online and it's invaluable to have that time to talk through my anxieties and help me rationalise them. I'm talking to my friends and family about how I'm feeling which is helping and also limiting the amount of news I watch or read and baking or being creative instead.

Naomi, 21, said:

> I've been feeling really anxious about what's going on at the moment. My normal coping strategies such as keeping a routine, getting out of the house and meeting people are now no longer possible and this is a big trigger for my existing anxiety which is getting worse. What would normally be quite a stressful time in my final year of university is harder at the moment. I've found some coping strategies are helping, such as making a journal to check in with my emotions, lots of self-care and setting a goal of a certain number of people to interact with each day.

Laughter often helps, and cartoonists all over the world have been inspired by the virus. Two examples are worth noting. In Hong Kong, an illustration by Ah To shows a person keeping toilet paper in their safe along with their gold bars and surgical masks. There is also a set of Chinese cartoons by Sadan that beautifully sums up the virus's life in China. In the first part, subdued yet anxious citizens in surgical masks are going about their day-to-day lives. In the second part, doctors grapple with a grim reaper, fighting vigorously to stop the virus from spreading. In the final part, demons are running amok, a depiction of what awaits if the virus wins.

I believe laughter is also useful as it helps build up resilience in a crisis.

Resilience

The way people respond to any kind of trauma depends on the extent of their resilience. The concept is not hard to illustrate. A boxer is hit and falls on to the floor. One man may simply give up at that point, while a second slugger shakes his head, gets up and carries on fighting.

In 2017, Suniya Luthar of Arizona State University and her colleague Nancy Eisenberg, PhD, published a special section in *Child Development* to highlight what can help promote resilience in families and children (2017). The virus crisis makes some of their findings instructive.

In one brief home-visit program, for instance, parents were helped to develop skills for becoming more positive and effective dealing with their children. They were taught to praise the children more and punish them less. The parents themselves got considerable support and were referred for additional family-based interventions. Parents who took part showed more positive parenting behaviours and fewer depressive symptoms. Their children showed fewer social and emotional problems as did the children whose mothers attended weekly group sessions led by trained supervisors at early childhood agencies.

Increasing access to such programs could have a significant effect on public health by improving health and wellbeing in childhood and beyond, Morris and her co-authors (2017) conclude. The lead author is an associate editor of the *Journal of Research into Adolescence*. By partnering with community sites – such as paediatric clinics and Head Start centres – the programs could be scaled up to reach large numbers of at-risk families, they say. A lesson to remember. A variety of research has also shown that treating maternal depression can trickle down to improve children's mental health. Goodman and Garber (2017) reviewed programs that involved interpersonal therapy or cognitive-behavioural therapy (CBT) strategies to manage maternal depression and improve parenting and found both in-home programs and those administered through sites such as child care or community health centres improved parenting skills.

Chapter 8

Introspection is inevitable

Mood regulation, dreams and personal responses

No one since the virus hit has talked much about people suffering from time stress, from having too much to do in their busy lives as they juggle work, family and so-called me time while rushing from meeting to meeting or airport to airport.

An ironic gift of the virus is time, since so much of the usual frenzy has been put on hold. This chapter looks at how we can use this time well.

Use this isolation as an opportunity to introspect. Ask yourself serious questions:

What do I really like?
What will make me feel good when life returns to normal?

We all like secrets. What will make me feel happy, but my knife, bushand, spabner doesn't know I like. These aren't misprints but deliberate mistakes, to jog you into seeing things slightly differently. Obviously the words should read wife, husband, partner.

Most advice on survival stresses staying positive. Hope is a good drug but many people realise that being nothing but an optimist is unrealistic, so they steel themselves to explore and even embrace their dark side. We all have a dark side – Freud and Jung agreed on that. A dark side of hate, fear, desire for revenge. I believe we need to confront that when we are left alone or with just one or two people.

Dare to think uncomfortable thoughts you have avoided before:

Who do you dislike in your family?
Who do you resent professionally?
Who do you hate because they rejected you emotionally or sexually?
What do you think you could have done differently in those situations?

Presence makes love grow less fond

Most of us do not spend 24 hours a day with those we love. So much time together may well bring out flaws in the relationship. This is a very difficult issue. The literature on separation and divorce covers many cases where people continue living together even though the relationship has become Arctic. There is a 1950 comedy where Dad tells the children to tell Mum to pass the salt because he can't bring himself to talk to her. This part of the chapter will look at a number of such case histories and at how people coped – or failed to cope – with them.

In our isolation situation, try to remember the fact that you are not in an interminable quandary, as this will end. It seems sensible to take the temperature of your relationship sometimes when you are isolated. Honesty is not easy, but avoiding how you feel will not improve your feelings.

Study your face

Gaze at yourself in the mirror. We will all have time to spend in the bathroom and the bathroom may be the one place you can be alone. Let your imagination roam into every corner of your self. Write your thoughts down in a diary immediately, as we often forget what is uncomfortable and we repress it without even knowing we repress it. This exercise will help you when you are plunged into the dark, as we all will be at times during this crisis.

Introspection should make you more aware of your moods, which will vary during the day. Guy Goodwin and colleagues in a study in *JAMA* (Taquet et al., 2020) examined a selection of activities that people may use as a form of mood regulation to stave off depression. He argued,

> When we are down, we tend to choose to do things that cheer us up, and when we are up, we may take on activities that will tend to bring us down. However, in our current situation with COVID-19, lockdowns, and social isolation, our choice of activity is very limited.

He and his colleagues analysed the histories of 58,328 participants, comparing those with low mood (depression) and high mood. His team tracked the extent to which people responded to their moods through their choice of activities throughout the day. In rich countries, people were more likely to choose exercise for mood regulation. In lower-income populations, individuals were more likely to choose religious activities, which shows how we can behave just as they did in mediaeval Europe when fighting the Black Death. They found a significant link between rarely or never practising this form of mood regulation and depression. The less you tried to control your moods, the more depressed you were liable to become.

Goodwin notes, "Our research shows this normal mood regulation is impaired in people with depression, providing a new, direct target for further research and development of new treatments to help people with depression" (Taquet et al., 2020). He added that choosing activities that basically perk you up seemed able to prevent or better treat depression. This is likely to be important at times of lockdown and social isolation.

Introspection also involves thinking about your dreams – and there is evidence that people are now remembering more of their dreams. This seems paradoxical, but I argue for an explanation. My speculation owes much to Michel Jouvet, a towering figure in dream research who I interviewed for my book *Psychologists on Psychology*.

Dreams

Jouvet, of the University of Lyon, worked on cats and found that a structure in the brainstem called the pons governed their rapid eye movement (REM) sleep. The pons is responsible for basic biological functions, like breathing and sensory perception; by contrast, the cortex, a higher brain region, governs conscious thought and actions.

Jouvet's discovery suggested that REM sleep could continue without the involvement of higher brain structures and that it had an important biological function even for animals with little capacity for reasoning. He called the REM state 'paradoxical sleep', since the brain is active even though the body is virtually still. When the cats were deprived of the pons they could move and then they acted out their dreams, which were usually horribly aggressive.

"Dreaming became the third state of the brain, as different from sleep as sleep was from waking," Jouvet (1999) wrote in *The Paradox of Sleep: The Story of Dreaming*. Research has since confirmed that human beings have brain structures that govern REM sleep similar to those found in cats. Most warm-blooded animals, like mammals and birds, have periods of REM sleep. (Dolphins and many species of whales are notable exceptions.) Jouvet told me:

> In an adult I believe the effects of not dreaming will be subtle but could be dangerous. Let me make an analogy. In *Clockwork Orange* the 'hero' Alex Delarge is a thug and is subjected to a Skinner-type programme which conditioned him to be disgusted with Beethoven. The technique was simple aversion. He would watch films which had much music. He becomes a boy. He hates Beethoven's music. Then the boy falls from a window and says "I had a dream" when he wakes up.

Jouvet found this ingenious and argued that the suppression of dreams made us more susceptible to being moulded as "the individual becomes more conditionable".

Jouvet believed that REM sleep somehow allowed the basic genetic code that made up our personality to replay and refresh itself. Rob me of my dreams and you rob me of myself, he suggested. If that is so, why are we dreaming more, as a survey conducted by King's College London (King's College Survey) suggests? Sixty-two percent of people in the UK are getting just as much sleep, if not more, than before social distancing measures.

Mark Blagrove, a psychologist at Swansea University, argues that when you sleep for longer, you have more rapid eye movement sleep. He states that time-poor modern life, however, typically involves shortened sleep and may be leading to an 'epidemic' of dream loss. That may now be changing for some. "Lack of work schedules may be allowing individuals to wake up without an alarm clock," say Blagrove et al. (2019). "Natural wake-ups are known to result in longer dreams."

Blagrove's work suggests that talking about your dreams can alleviate distress and lead to greater empathy and social bonding. He argues that we should not worry about our dreams but take comfort in the fact that your brain is doing what it should be doing. In fact, if you accept Jouvet's idea that when we dream we somehow replay the genetic code that makes us who we are, dreaming more may be a brilliant defence mechanism. It cements our sense of ourselves. That may be useful if we feel under attack.

Some dreams reflect that feeling clearly. Deirdre Barrett, a dream researcher and assistant professor of psychology at Harvard University, is collecting pandemic-related dreams, after studying the dreams of survivors of 11 September 2001 and British prisoners of World War II. A crisis like this 'stirs up our dreams', whether this means you experience more vivid dreams, more emotional dreams or more bizarre dreams (Barrett, 2020).

She has created an online survey where people can record dreams they feel are about the pandemic, with about 7,000 dreams submitted so far by about 2,800 respondents. Barrett already has a sense of the trends. "There are these anxiety dreams about 'I'm getting it,'" she says. One major category is bug-attack dreams, in which insects stand in for the virus. There are also lots of invisible monsters, reflecting the fact the virus is invisible too. People who are lonely may find themselves on Mars or in prison, whereas those who feel too crowded at home may dream the entire neighbourhood has moved in.

Barrett also says your last quarter of sleep provides about half of your dreaming time – "and the most vivid dreams". And because you may not be rushing headfirst into a busy routine like you used to, you may have a greater chance of mentally hanging onto those dreams.

Freud spent years trying to understand dream interpretation, but now psychologists are even offering advice on how to avoid bad dreams or to shake off the haunting feeling they leave you with. Barrett suggests that upon awakening you redirect your attention to "something good that you know you're going to be able to do that day, that you can look forward to". Some psychologists even suggest rewriting the dream, trying to change or finish the dream in a positive way. "Rehearsing the nightmare while awake could cause a more positive outcome the next time that one has the same dream," Erin Wamsley, who runs the dream lab at Furman University, told the *Washington Post*.

Barrett encourages people to be open to the possibility that their bad dreams are symptomatic of unacknowledged concerns. "Once you consciously understand something", she says, "the emotion usually lets up." But like many psychologists, she believes the individual can exert more control than one might imagine. She suggests that instead of coping with the aftermath of bad dreams, you could try ordering up some better ones. As you are falling asleep, "come up with something you're really excited about in a positive way," Barrett says. "Tell yourself, 'I want to dream about this tonight.'" In a study she conducted with 76 college students, half were able to influence their dreams using this method.

The study of the dreams of this period may well show that our unconscious has become more transparent in revealing its anxieties than in Freud's day. A paradox of the virus.

Panic in pandemics

We live in a quick-response world. Reicher et al. (2020) did not ponder for months and provided a dichotomy of how psychology responded weeks after the pandemic started. They spoke of one view that people are "fragile rationalists who, however, find it hard to handle complex information and to deal with risk and uncertainty." Under pressure they stop thinking rationally. "We let our emotions get the better of us, so we panic. We saw this when people stripped supermarket shelves."

A tiny detail. One of my group of 35 admitted to me that his wife bought 1,600 toilet paper rolls early on. However, recent unpublished data mentioned by Reicher suggests that stockpilers are a tiny percentage of the population and the real reason for shortages is the fragile 'just in time' supply chains of modern supermarkets.

Reicher and his two colleagues continued that if people are so child-like in a crisis, they need the government to look after them. But in Britain the government worried people would not accept rules. Since I am a psychologist, I will speculate as to the unconscious anxieties in Downing Street. Our rulers fretted because they knew the government were hardly persons of the people. The prime minister is an Old Etonian – which used to be *de rigeur* to get into Downing Street until Wilson, Heath, Callaghan, Thatcher and Major did so. The current prime minister's chief adviser has a father-in-law who lives in a castle. Strict distancing measures were delayed apparently because the government feared people would soon be 'fatigued' and stop observing them. In fact, this did not happen much until late May, after Dominic Cummings breached the lockdown rules and when the lovely weather made people flock to beaches.

According to Reicher et al. (2020), the second psychological view is that people are much more competent and able to make sense of the crisis. It is

> constructive in the sense that we don't distort information but rather create meaning and understanding with the tools available to us, and also constructive in the sense that we are well able to cope with our world, even in crisis.

They also deploy the idea that collectivity creates resilience in crises. "When people think of themselves as 'we' rather than 'I' that they are most likely to accept measures that optimise the overall fight against coronavirus" – even at considerable cost. And people have had to accept not being at the bedside of someone they love who is dying.

Reicher et al. (2020) finally contrast "a psychology which is at odds with the medical advice, which is counterposed to systemic interventions and which both disrespects and dismisses those who are best able to respond to this crisis" with a psychology that is focused "on how best to implement the medical advice, which advocates for systemic change that makes optimal behaviours possible, and which harnesses the power of the group to face up to COVID-19."

My initial group of 35 tended to be positive rather than panicky, as this selection of responses shows. They provide nothing more than a snapshot of how people have responded.

Responses from my 35

M wrote:

I am 70 years old and live by myself. I enjoy very good health, am active, eat fairly healthily and only drink in moderation.

I consider myself to be extremely fortunate in these circumstances. In terms of tangible things, I have a house, a garden, an income and a full larder. This is not so for many, perhaps most others and I find it hard to bear how this is affecting our most vulnerable children. My brother and his family live close by and although I don't see them they are in almost daily contact. I have excellent neighbours – who offer to shop, bring me food etc. – a realisation that they think I am old! I am not technically very skilled but have learned to join a meeting, Zoom, Facetime, WhatsApp and play Bridge Base Online.

As a child, my family lived in Venezuela – I say this as I think it in some way prepared me for these times. My school was very isolated, each day/week was like the ones before and as I only went home once a year, I learned to maintain and sustain relationships at a distance. Of course I wish it was different and I could meet with family and friends, but I refuse to grumble.

S was far less cheerful:

Happy to be 'consulted', but not sure what I've got to contribute. Long rants about austerity, Brexit, social care . . . ? Am busy with the usual Zoom/Skype/WhatsApp events, plus local Residents' Assoc, and am trustee of local grant-giving charity, trying to support domestic abuse and food banks, plus individual grants where possible. We also have some almshouses – actually 17 tiny flats in an old church building – which worry me to death. So far no infections thank goodness, and an amazing warden to rely on. Also am one of the NHS responders – but like the other

749,999 volunteers have never been contacted. Otherwise gardening, running and eating and drinking too much. We are just so lucky to have space, food, money etc., though I realise many of you will have medical conditions to worry about.

A former director of social services wrote:

I thought I was taking lockdown in my stride until my friend fell sick with a serious bladder infection. It sent her crazy and trying to organise a urine test, the right medication, and eventually a hospital admission all proved hugely difficult and necessitated many visits – a 15-mile round trip each time. Then on discharge setting up a full care package and making sure she had suitable food for the micro-wave – which I also had to purchase – required even more frequent visits and phone calls. Her nearby son is elderly and shielded for his own health, so unable to help. It's so sad to see such an independent woman be so completely alone and now she is clearly suffering a complete mental collapse. She was readmitted to hospital this morning and I'm fearful for what is to happen next. The worst thing is not to be able to see her there.

Another social worker wrote:

Apart from the theme of 'neglectful thinking' regarding older people in care homes, I am struck by the different whole systems yardstick! As I recall my days as direc-tor, trying to come to terms with managing a whole system over which I had little direct control, politicians were very demanding! We were expected to operate it like a machine – push a button here, pull a lever there and bingo, reduce delayed discharges and admissions to residential care, while lowering front end demands on the NHS to boot. No time for any of the complexities/structural impediments that we faced or the need to keep the rest of the SSD show on the road – these were seen largely as excuses.

W wrote:

Very different now, politicians have a similar responsibility – an army of people at their disposal and all else is shelved, as they panic and huffpuff on very short-term aims that give an impression of progress (for a while). I don't want to be too hard on them in difficult times but if Hancock's pursuit of an arbitrary testing figure (and his changing of the goalposts) is the measure of their understanding and integrity, they fail miserably.

We need to think longer term; green shoots on the value of social care are emerg-ing, we must cultivate them and use the coming period to raise them further and embed them.

F wrote:

I hope you are managing to keep sane in this extended lockdown. When I sent out a newsletter 8 weeks ago, I naïvely thought that things might be slowly coming back to normal by now. . . . At home in London, we've realised that we have to tighten up our daily routine for the long haul; everyone was working hard, but we were still in GMT and the children still in pyjamas at the end of the day! So now we're getting out of the house first thing in the morning to try and regain some structure.

R pointed to what helped:

And as life unfolds, music is certainly one of the things that is keeping us positive. There's been a lot of reminiscing about old albums and meaningful music from our past. So I'm glad that my forthcoming Concertos album features an older piece that many of you may already be familiar with: my Concerto for Turntables No.1 – this time is in its symphonic version (commissioned for the Proms back in 2011). It's partnered with my Cello Concerto which has yet to be performed outside Russia, so I expect this will be new for most of you. Two singles have already been released digitally, but the CD is worth getting if you still have a player;-) – more details below.

On the day of release there will be a livestream launch party with both the amazing soloists performing live from London and Moscow. I'll be hosting, making toasts, DJ-ing and piping a party atmosphere into your homes.

I really hope you can join us for that (info below).

A performance artist wrote:

Corona'ed

My entire career has been spent in the gig economy of live theatre, cabaret and festivals. My trademark is 'hands-on comedian', getting up close and personal with the audience (whether they like it or not). Before The Virus I was known as a button-pusher; climbing on people, sitting in laps, kissing and occasionally licking. Now all that I am, professionally at least, has been erased, put on indefinite hold, skewered by the unforgiving spikes of the corona virus.

I managed to get out of Copenhagen where I had been on contract just before lockdown. Back in London I sat in fallow shock for a couple of weeks then rejoined my community in online shows on Zoom and Facebook. But without the immediacy of a live audience, the gasps, laughter and heckles, we come up short every time. The internet seems to be the only thing holding the locked down world together right now, but for live artists Covid-19 is a dangerous economic limbo from which we may never recover.

A friend, J, said:

Lockdown has not been that bad. I have mixed with a small group of people who have only been in contact with our group. This group has now expanded. I have been out everyday shopping, walking and cycling.

The rest of the family are different. They don't need to get out. My wife is happy in her office, moving from there only to get to bed and an occasional sortie to the kitchen. The children don't get up until 2 pm. Then either online school or Netflix. Life is not too bad. Travel and restaurants are the thing I miss the most.

T, who lives in Venice, told me he was fed up. His wife was in Rome and they had been separated for weeks. He found the situation frustrating not just because they were apart but also because no one knew when restrictions would be lifted and life might return to normal – and what the so-called new normal might be. He was lucky in that he owned a vineyard and could wander through it.

E has spent much of his time turning his small garden into a bit of a jewel while he waits for a transplant. It has helped him cope with anxiety, as he has become unemployed.

N has been ill and has become very worried because he cannot sleep, and he is anxious he will get the virus. My sample – largely people who have not been too affected by economic anxieties – does show how some of us, at least, are using the crisis to think.

Chapter 9

Money fears and how to cope with them

Connecting financial security and mental health

Economics is known as the 'dismal science', but few non-economists know the dismal origin of the saying. The phrase was first used in Thomas Carlyle's 1849 tract *Occasional Discourse on the Negro Question*, where he argued slavery should be reintroduced because the freed men were not working as productively as before in the West Indies. The "idle Black man in the West Indies" should be "*compelled* to work as he was fit, and to *do* the Maker's will who had constructed him", Carlyle thundered.

Carlyle went on to explain that economics was "not a 'gay science', I should say, like some we have heard of; no, a dreary, desolate and, indeed, quite abject and distressing one; what we might call, by way of eminence, the *dismal science*."

One hundred seventy years on, economics has never been as dismal as it is now, as a cascade of figures, forecasts and algorithms tumble out of every official orifice to predict how much the world economy will shrink. The poor house awaits. For most of us the problems will be personal – and obvious.

> Will I keep my job?
> Will I have to take a much lower paid and lower status job?
> What help is there if I am made redundant?
> How will I manage my debts?
> How can I make sure I get every benefit I am entitled to?
> Will I have to use food banks?
> Are there other forms of help I can turn to – and where can I access them?

A quick note on financial shame first. Many of us when we are in financial trouble feel ashamed and do not like to talk about it or ask for help. In normal times, to ring the building society to explain why you have not made the monthly payment is difficult. Everyone else is up to date. You have always been up to date so far. If you miss three payments, you get a visit from an inspector of expenditure who asks you to justify every penny you spend. If you don't satisfy her or him, you will soon be homeless as your house is repossessed. In America during the Global Financial Crisis of

2008–2009, many people lost their houses because they could not pay the mortgage.

The situation is different now. The world is facing a financial crisis and it does need putting in some – yes – dismal context.

Forecasts of the fall in global GDP yo-yo from the bad to the catastrophic. People in the UK, the US and, just to pick at random, India are losing jobs at a rate never seen before. As the government warned of lockdown, India saw hundreds of thousands of people who worked in New Delhi start to walk back to their native villages. They would get fed there at least.

The study of the relationship between unemployment and mental health started in 1930. Marie Jahoda (1933), her husband Paul Lazarsfeld and Hans Zeisel conducted a survey of Marienthal, a small town of 1,500 in Austria. The methodology was simple. They talked to many people and asked questions about how they felt and what they feared. The town's textile factory closed, causing mass unemployment. Individuals who had lost their work and their wages sank into despair and social misery. The authors observed that "no one lives for the community anymore, food is running out, it is rationed, and neglected people no longer listen to the radio, no longer read the newspapers and let the city slowly disintegrate."

People consumed less meat and bought fewer clothes. They became more isolated as they took part in fewer social activities and even borrowed fewer books from the local library. This even affected, the authors claimed, the way their subjects experienced time. Going to work gives our days – and therefore time – structure. When they had no work to go to in Marienthal, those who lived there felt their awareness of time was fading and they could no longer accurately describe how they spent their days. "We can thus read that they conclude that 'unemployment is a poisoned gift', because they do not manage to use their new free time," the authors concluded. It also led to a feeling "of moral uselessness".

Strangely, this seminal book was not translated into English in the 1930s when there was mass unemployment. In the 1960s, in Sheffield, Peter Warr (2001) studied the relationship between unemployment and mental health. Being out of work damaged wellbeing, behaviour and attitudes. In the 1980s, unemployment rose steeply.

The Department of Employment said the number of people claiming unemployment benefits in the UK soared to 2.1 million in April 2020, the first full month of the coronavirus lockdown. In the United States in May 2020, 30 million people were unemployed, the *Washington Post* reported on 6 June, after 1.9 million more claimants signed on during May.

In its April 2020 outlook report, the International Monetary Fund (2020) projected global growth in 2020 to fall to –3%. This would make the Great Lockdown the worst recession since the Great Depression, and the Global Financial Crisis just a small dip. Industries such as tourism, travel, hospitality and entertainment have been disrupted and will take long to recover. Business travel may fare worse as companies see there is less need for expensive trips when you can do work via Zoom. Economists can rarely be precise in their predictions because they have to juggle so many different complex data.

Since there is a personal element to this book, I can say I have been a victim of what we might call the end of travel. I have two houses in London which I let out through Airbnb. Every booking from March to the end of July 2020 was cancelled. Airbnb has made something like 7,000 staff redundant. In an unusual example of capitalist generosity, however, the company is giving hosts 25% of the rents they would have received if the virus had not stopped all travel plans. My tiny Airbnb enterprise had no full-time staff, but two people helped. Maria let guests in and out at sometimes very unsocial hours, while Tina did some cleaning. Now there are no guests to let in and no guests to clean after.

The British Library provides access to a site endorsed by MIND which offers advice on how to work from home. "The number one thing to remember from this talk is that you need to look after yourself before it gets to breaking point" (2020). It advises a number of ways of doing this which are summarized below:

- Add structure, i.e., take a lunch break even if you are by yourself at home
- Leave home at home and work at work, which is admittedly tricky when working at home, but try setting boundaries
- Eat, sleep and exercise; it's not about quantity, it's about quality
- Celebrate little wins
- Rethink rejection
- Add YOU to the to-do list
- Try to open up
- Have a Wellbeing Action Plan – if you are your own boss, have one for yourself as your 'employee'

This is all sensible advice, but it does not deal with the spectre of unemployment, which today provokes much anxiety. Muenster et al. (2011) suggested that while the effect that reducing job insecurity has on mental health is rather vague, there is evidence that such policies benefit the most vulnerable group, i.e., those that are already in poor mental health.

Predictions only contribute to uncertainty. For all its gravitas, the International Monetary Fund does not pretend its predictions are certain. It claims that if the pandemic fades in the second half of 2020 and the policy actions taken around the globe do help prevent bankruptcies and major job losses, global growth in 2021 should rebound to 5.8%. But it is far from sure the policy actions will work. So keep the champagne on ice.

The International Monetary Fund (2020) boasts, "we are actively deploying our 1-trillion-dollar lending capacity to support vulnerable countries, including through rapid-disbursing emergency financing and debt service relief to our poorest member countries, and we are calling on official bilateral creditors to do the same."

The dismal science gushes with some figures that are so gigantic – like this $1 trillion lending capacity – they are hard to make sense of unless perhaps you have qualified in the dismal science. It is easier to make sense of life-sapping redundancies. The BBC and ITN, among many other media outlets, listed the British companies that have announced redundancies; the list certainly makes dismal reading, including:

Jaguar
Rolls Royce
JCB
Ovo Energy

British Airways announced 12,000 jobs would go, but reduced that drastically after trade union and government pressure (BBC News, 2020). Sales of new cars in up to May 2020 were down by 89%, back to the level of 1952. Ryanair, possibly the most bullish of airlines, claims they will fly 80 million passengers this year instead of 130 million. In May, however, they flew 70,000 passengers, a staggering fall of 99.5% from their forecast. Even agile internet operators like BuzzFeed have had to lay off staff.

By offering various schemes for paying the wages of employees, the Chancellor of the Exchequer has tried to protect the jobs of as many people as possible. In March 2020, the British government also told people to work from home if possible. The government daily briefing on the virus estimated that 60% of workers are at home, but it is not clear if that estimate includes those who are 'furloughed'. Working from home is not something you can do if you work in a pub or a restaurant or a hairdresser's or drive a bus or serve in a shop. The government allowed shops to open on 15 June provided they follow strict rules to keep shoppers 2 metres separate and went in for continuous cleaning. Many shops did not manage to comply.

It is easy to say the main issues facing most of us are how to survive during the lockdown and whether there will there be a job for us when the pandemic is over. But how do you do it?

It usually helps to divide the problem into segments. Instead of fretting about finances, consider each issue in turn:

What can you do about your rent or mortgage?
What can you about utility bills?
How much do you need to spend on essentials?

When people are in financial trouble, they often find it hard to confront the facts and they hide. Don't, especially now, as the whole world is in financial trouble.

At the time of writing, homeowners have the option of asking for a mortgage holiday, which may be three to six months long. Interest will be charged as the debt grows, but buying time is useful. While mortgage ads say your home is at risk if you don't keep up repayments, the government has also ruled out homes being repossessed until October 2020. So, if you're reading this hot off the press, contact your mortgage lender and ask for a holiday.

Parliament is protecting renters from eviction through the Coronavirus Act 2020. All new evictions are suspended and landlords cannot bring new possession proceedings to obtain possession of their property. Housing associations and local authorities also will not be allowed to evict tenants who are affected by coronavirus and do not pay their rent.

Alok Sharma (2020), the business secretary, brought in measures to help households that "need additional support and reassurance". The government insisted that no customers should be cut off from utilities during the lockdown. Yet energy suppliers are continuing to use debt collectors to chase unpaid bills, after promising to help households during the coronavirus pandemic by offering payment plans to struggling customers.

A letter sent by a debt collector on behalf of Shell Energy and reported in *The Guardian* on 26 April warns one customer that a doorstep collector may visit their home in order to chase an outstanding balance of £78.51. It warned that Shell Energy would share the account holder's details with credit reference agencies.

The UK's largest energy suppliers, British Gas and Ovo Energy, said they were continuing to use debt collectors, but not to collect monies as in the past. Both companies said they had instructed their debt collectors to offer financial help on their behalf. The agencies were "only used as a last-resort attempt to engage with a customer and only after we've repeatedly asked them to get in contact to see how we can help".

In the US, companies such as CenterPoint Energy, Xcel Energy and Minnesota Power have announced they won't shut off customers' power if they're unable to pay at this time.

Check whether your utility company has already announced exceptions for payments online. If so, call up the company to tell them about your situation. You can still give them a call if you can't find any information about special circumstances online. It's possible they're still willing to work with you.

Information overload is also an issue, as there are many possible sources of help. The most useful general site I have found is Grantfinder, which provides good information on where to apply. If you don't ask, you won't get.

Being shy is not a good tactic – and if you are at all prone to depression, grit your teeth and ask. Then reward yourself because you have been brave enough to face the problem and try to do something about it. Economics may be dismal. You don't have to be.

Chapter 10

My home is my office

Working from home as the new normal?

The government tells us to work from home if at all possible, as the prime minister does at 10 Downing Street. Home working will stop us from being too close to strangers, more so as we will not be commuting. A study of European nations (Eurostat European Commission News Release, 2018) in 2018 found that only 15% of people worked from home, and that included freelancers. The Netherlands topped the list with 35%. No one has accurate figures now, partly because at the time of writing so many people have been furloughed until normal life resumes. Nurses, doctors, drivers and farmers, among many others, will have to work from bus depots, surgeries and the land as usual.

We live in so many different configurations – alone, with partners, with partners and children, back in the house of mum and dad because something has gone awry, with flat mates – and managing to work from home will differ in each one. In some of these cases you will need to consult, negotiate and agree. If you are on the phone to a client, anyone else in the room will have to be quiet.

If you have to work from home, don't just slide into it. It's a big change and if you live with your family, it is one that will involve everyone, to a certain extent. So make discussing it an event, an occasion. Sit round the table, get in cakes and nice drinks. And remember this is a decision the whole family needs to go along with.

If you are going to have to change the way your home is arranged, it's not just up to you. You need to discuss this with your spouse or partner and with the children and stepchildren. Words matter, but pictures matter too – and can be more fun.

Redesign your home:

> Get hold of a number of coloured pencils and crayons.
> Draw a map of your home as it is.
> Draw a map of how you would like to change it and explain why.
> Give everyone else the chance to show how they would like to change it and to explain why.

Remember that dedicated space in which you can work is not a luxury, as to keep going, we have to work.

Give children the chance to suggest ways to make your work space cosier or more fun.

Finally, set rules, especially under what conditions you can be interrupted.

If a child feels sick, that's a good reason to interrupt, but if 4-year-old Ben cannot find his Tyrannosaurus rex which he last saw under the sofa, retrieving the dinosaur can wait till you stop for lunch. In crises some of us get quirky, so do not be tempted to tease children by hiding all their dinosaurs, sharks or dolls because you are in a grump yourself.

Given that we will have time, this book is peppered with ideas for films to watch. The wonderful 1950s film *The Apartment* with Jack Lemmon and Shirley MacLaine is set in an insurance company, where hundreds of employees toil in one huge hangar-like space, use the same elevators, the same canteens and the same toilets, unless they are big chiefs and cheeses who have special facilities. Working from home will avoid all these risks.

When you have to clock in at work by 8.30 a.m., you know the routine. Get up, have breakfast, say goodbye to the family, drive off or get the tube or bus to work. These routines no longer exist, so we need willpower to stop us lazing in bed and starting our day at 9 a.m. instead of 7 a.m., and then deciding to enjoy the kind of slow breakfast we normally have on weekends.

In Holland, which was one of the cradles of capitalism, some people go out the front door, leave their domestic space and walk round to their back door to enter their work space. It's a slightly obsessive demarcation, but Holland actually home schools more of its children than any other European country. This odd routine may help by giving clear divides.

If you work from home, you will have to stay in touch with colleagues and clients by WhatsApp, Zoom and other apps. We all need reassurance that other people are still breathing out there – emails do not quite give that. If you are becoming a phone or Skype person, brush up your phone manner and etiquette. The following 'rules' may seem simplistic, but are still useful to remember:

Introduce yourself the moment the phone is answered.

Ask how the other person is doing. The Hungarian humourist George Mikes in his brilliant *How To Be an Alien* (1946) said no one really expected a proper answer, but he was writing in 1946. This is a different moment and we need to show we are listening.

Agree on the topics you will discuss.

Do not interrupt them.

If you really can't understand, then be very polite in asking them to repeat the point.

Smooth talk may help things go smoothly.

Thank those you have talked to at the end of the call.

There will still be office politics and jealousies. Depending on how large the group is where you work, try to develop tactics where these can be parked. Things will be tough enough without turf wars as to who gets to their name first on that important report to the board. Try also to include moments of celebration when your company pulls off a nice deal or just gets through the day.

The physical

Ask yourself if you have found the best position from which to work. I had a neighbour once who held a senior job but liked to wander in his shorts when taking business calls. He was smart. A 2011 study in *Diabetologia* showed that the average adult spent 50–60% of their day in sedentary pursuits (Wilmot et al., 2011). Those who spent the most time sitting were at risk, as the longest time spent on the bum was associated with a

- 112% increase in risk of diabetes
- 147% increase in cardiovascular events
- 90% increase in deaths due to cardiovascular events
- 49% increase in deaths due to any cause.

National Health Service (NHS) Guidelines offer ideas on how to make the best of sitting down:

> Don't sit in the same position in the same chair for long periods. Change your posture as often as is practicable. We easily get used to the same old chair, which actually makes us stiff.
> Reduce your risk of back pain by adjusting your chair, so your lower back is well supported.
> Adjust the height of your chair so you can use your computer keyboard with your wrists and forearms straight and level with the floor.
> Place your feet flat on the floor. If they're not, get a footrest, which lets you rest your feet at a level that's comfortable.
> Don't cross your legs, as this may harm your posture.
> Your screen should be in front of you. Put the monitor about an arm's length away, with the top of the screen roughly at eye level. If you need a monitor stand, get one. If the screen is too high or too low, you'll have to bend your neck, which will get uncomfortable during a working day.
> Rest your wrists often.

The guidelines also advise that if you phone a lot at work, you should exchange your handset for a headset. Repeatedly cradling the phone between your ear and shoulder can strain your neck muscles.

One of the top researchers in this field, James Levine (2015) of the Mayo Clinic, studied a group of office workers. He added 1,000 calories to their daily intake and told them not to change any exercise or movement habits. Some of the workers gained weight, while others did not. Curious as to what was making the difference, Levine and his team sewed sensors into the knickers of the workers to track their movements. The group not gaining weight spent far less time sitting. The group that did not gain sat 2.25 hours less than their colleagues.

So the physical lesson is to move as much as possible while making yourself comfortable. A weird jumping nugget, meanwhile. Droplets from a sneeze can outperform Olympic long jumpers: a top-class sneeze can fly 9 metres, which is 5 centimetres more than the world record long jump held by Mike Powell.

The psychological lesson is to analyse what makes you irritable and how you make others irritable, since working from home means sharing the space. That requires being open and honest, so you know some trigger points best avoided.

Chapter 11

Exercise your endorphins
How physical activity can affect mood

The living rooms of newly built homes in Britain are nearly a third smaller than equivalent homes built in the 1970s, according to research that charts how living space has shrunk to levels last seen 80 years ago. The research, by LABC Warranty (https://www.labcwarranty.co.uk/), which provides warranties for new-build homes, found the average living room in a house built since 2010 was 17.1 square metres (184 square feet), compared with 24.9 square metres (268 square feet) in the 1970s, a 32% contraction.

In the 1950s the ethologist John Calhoun wanted to see how overcrowding would influence social behaviour in rats. He placed rats in a confined space and allowed them to multiply with relatively little control. The results looked like scenes out of a horror movie: cannibalism, dead infants and complete social withdrawal, to name a few.

Calhoun's rats captured the public imagination and inspired a surge of research on the psychological effects of density in our own species. Some studies found that people living in crowded environments indeed showed a variety of social pathologies, just like Calhoun's rats. But other studies did not. Reviews of the early research concluded that popular fears about overcrowding may be unfounded. Solari and Mare (2012) showed the effects on children. For them, living in a crowded home damages wellbeing. They claimed that every extra person per room decreased math and reading test scores by 2.1 and 2.0 percentage points, respectively. And as the home was more crowded, children's behaviour problems increased and they tended to be more withdrawn, depressed or bad tempered.

Research on how we survive lockdown will show if that still stands. One person who will not be affected is the prime minister, especially as the Queen is letting him exercise in the somewhat extensive and not remotely over-crowded grounds of Buckingham Palace. As he goes through his routines, Mr Johnson will get plenty of chances to produce endorphins.

The discovery of endorphins was no accident. In the early 1970s, researchers were studying how opiates, such as heroin or morphine, affected the brain. They found that they interacted with specialised receptors in cells in the brain and spinal cord and hindered or blocked the transmission of pain signals. The word 'endorphin' actually comes from joining the words 'endogenous', meaning from within the body, and 'morphine', which is an opiate pain reliever. In other words, endorphins got their name because pain relief is one of their functions.

Endorphins are neurotransmitters, chemicals that help send signals from one neuron to the next. (A neuron is a brain cell.) They play a key role in the central nervous system and can either prompt or suppress nearby neurons to pass on the electrical signals that flow endlessly through our brains. They were first identified and named by two independent laboratories in the mid-1970s. In Scotland, John Hughes et al. (1977) isolated a small peptide sequence from the brain tissue of pigs and termed it 'enkephalin'. A peptide is a compound consisting of two or more amino acids linked in a chain. At the same time, investigators in the United States isolated an active molecule that seemed to work like morphine and called it 'endorphin'. The term 'endorphins' was used loosely in reference to cover peptides that had morphine-like properties. Now the term is used for many peptides that both reduce feelings of pain and can also cause euphoria.

Endorphins have generated so much buzz that I'm tempted to suggest Einstein's equation $E = mc^2$ should be re-written as EEE, where E stands for endorphins, eureka and Einstein.

When Einstein had his eureka moments, did he have an 'endorphin rush'? He left his brain to science and it has been analysed in great detail. Astonishingly, it seems to have been rather normal, though when he made his great breakthroughs, he probably endorphined like a fountain. A reasonable guess is that Mozart's brain produced the same gush.

Those of us who can't devise theories of relativity or write "The Magic Flute" can still get an endorphin rush from joy, sex and even a hot curry – especially with someone you fancy. You can still order food online. Laughter, as we shall see, also produces endorphins.

Endorphins seemed to act like a narcotic, reducing the perception of pain. The pain relief experienced as a result of their release has been claimed to be greater than that of morphine by Harber and Sutton (1984), and that has become the accepted view. Beta-endorphins have been the most studied and account for the majority of the data we have on these magical-seeming substances. Frequently, the runner's high experienced near the end of a long, challenging race is attributed to endorphin release and a surge of pain-relief peptides that block sensory receptors. Whether it is only β-endorphin molecules that cause this remains in debate. After years of work, no one is sure why this happens. One theory is that the brain perceives exercise as a type of pain, and therefore, it releases endorphins. Another theory is that the rise in fatty acids caused by exercise may make the blood more acidic, triggering endorphin release.

Many people imagine running is the only way to cause the release of endorphins. This is not true. It is a result of skewed sampling, as most research on exercise-induced neurotransmitter release has been performed on runners. Any form of aerobic exercise will release endorphins, in fact.

Until recently, it was not possible to measure endorphin levels in the human brain without harming the subject. However, new imaging methods make it possible to study the ebb and flow of endorphins as they interact with brain cells.

High endorphin concentrations induced by exercise have not just been linked to mood state changes, 'exercise-induced euphoria' and altered pain perception, but also to menstrual disturbances in female athletes. Some studies have also suggested that how we experience fatigue is affected by the release of endorphins. Simply put, you don't feel you are pushing yourself to your physiological limits because you are experiencing an endorphin rush.

Endorphins are involved in another puzzle. People with more friends have higher pain tolerance, Oxford University researchers have found. Katerina Johnson, an Oxford doctoral student, was studying whether differences in our neurobiology helped explain differences in depression (Johnson and Dunbar, 2016). In people who are depressed, the hippocampus in the brain – the region that helps regulate mood – is smaller. Exercise supports nerve cell growth in the hippocampus, which improves nerve cell connections, which helps relieve depression.

Luckily, there's no need to run an ultramarathon in order to increase endorphin levels in your brain. Simply enjoying a piece of dark chocolate, interacting with friends, playing music, meditating or watching your favourite TV shows can. The pleasure effect associated with endorphins is in part related to the increased dopamine production that occurs due to endorphin activity. Dopamine has many effects including boosting mood, enhancing body movement and helping the sympathetic nervous system, which directs how we respond to dangerous or stressful situations. A flash flood of hormones boosts the body's alertness and heart rate, sending extra blood to the muscles. Breathing quickens, delivering fresh oxygen to the brain, and an infusion of glucose is shot into the bloodstream for a quick energy boost.

Recently it has also become clear that endorphins play a role in the placebo effect. Just thinking that a medicine will relieve pain is enough to prompt the brain to release its own natural painkillers, a University of Michigan study has found. The Michigan study was the first to pinpoint a specific brain chemistry mechanism for a pain-related placebo effect. It may help explain why so many people feel they get relief from therapies and remedies that actually do nothing. The little green pills are inactive, and yet it helps to take them if you think they are true medicines. The results were published in the 24 August 2005 issue of the *Journal of Neuroscience* by a team from the University of Michigan's Molecular and Behavioural Neurosciences Institute (MBNI).

The Michigan research deals a serious blow to the idea that the placebo effect is a purely psychological, not physical, phenomenon, according to Arias-Reves and Zubieta-DeUrioste (2020) at the University of Michigan Medical School. They argued in an interview:

We were able to see that the endorphin system was activated in pain-related areas of the brain, and that activity increased when someone was told they were receiving a medicine to ease their pain. They then reported feeling less pain. The mind-body connection is quite clear.

The Michigan findings are based on brain scans from 14 young healthy men who agreed to allow researchers to inject their jaw muscles with a concentrated saltwater solution to cause pain. The injection was made while they were having their brains scanned by a positron emission tomography (PET) scanner. During one scan, they were told they would receive a medicine (in fact, a placebo) that might relieve pain. Every 15 seconds during the scans, they were asked to rate the intensity of their pain sensations on a scale of 0 to 100, and they gave more detailed first-person ratings after the experiment. The researchers correlated the subjects' ratings with their PET scans and found how the placebo worked – again, an endorphin effect.

Laughing also causes a release of these seemingly magical substances. "Very little research has been done into why we laugh and what role it plays in society," according to Robin Dunbar (Welsh, 2011) of the University of Oxford. "We think that it is the bonding effects of the endorphin rush that explain why laughter plays such an important role in our social lives." The first basic test was to see if laughter causes an endorphin release. They tested subjects for their pain threshold, then showed them either funny material or something neutral. The subjects saw clips of *Mr Bean*, *Friends* and a live comedy show during the Edinburgh Fringe Festival. Laugh and the world laughs with you, they also found was true. Laughter was 30 times more likely to happen in a social context than when alone.

Sometimes psychology lets sadism bloom. The pain tests included wrapping a participant's arm in a frozen wine-cooling sleeve or a blood-pressure cuff. These tests were administered until the patient said they could not take it anymore. At the live shows, the researchers made subjects squat against a wall until they collapsed.

Across all tests, the participants could tolerate more pain after laughing. On average, watching about 15 minutes of comedy in a group increased pain threshold by 10%. Subjects tested alone showed slightly smaller increases in their pain threshold. On the other hand, when subjects watched an unfunny item, pain thresholds did not change (and were often lower). These results can best be explained by the action of endorphins released by laughter, Dunbar claims, and the way we breathe when we laugh is an important part of the explanation. The researchers believe that the long series of exhalations that accompany ribald laughter cause physical exhaustion of the abdominal muscles which, in turn, triggers endorphin release.

Interest in endorphins has also led to interest in endocannabinoids – chemical compounds that are naturally produced within the body and bind to the same brain receptors as compounds derived from cannabis (such as

THC, the principal psychoactive constituent). They reduce anxiety and make one feel more content partly because they increase dopamine in the brain's reward system. The biochemistry involved is complicated, but essentially endocannabinoids coordinate responses to seek, consume and store energy.

The most widely investigated endocannabinoid is anandamide (arachidonoyl ethanolamine [AEA]), initially isolated from the brain of pigs. Well-trained healthy volunteers who took part in a 'strenuous' hike at altitude below 2,100 metres and those who hiked and ascended approximately 2,000 metres in altitude both exhibited significant increases in circulating AEA concentrations following the exercise period (Feuerecker et al., 2012). Thirty to 90 minutes of moderate exercise also increases circulating concentrations of AEA (Heyman et al., 2012; Raichlen et al., 2013; Sparling et al., 2003).

In a new study in 2019, Jacob Meyer and researchers at the University of Wisconsin-Madison, Medical College of Wisconsin and William S. Middleton Memorial Veterans Hospital measured endocannabinoid levels and changes in mood before and after exercise sessions with varying levels of intensity. They found a significant boost in endocannabinoids and improvements in mood following prescribed moderate-intensity exercise. The findings are published in *Medicine & Science in Sports & Exercise*. Meyer says understanding the link between endocannabinoid levels, mood and exercise could lead to better treatment options for anxiety and depression.

Endocannabinoids also increase the pleasure we derive from being around others. If you are isolated with someone you love, exercise seems an excellent way to strengthen relationships. When spouses exercise together, both partners report more closeness later that day, according to Meyer et al. (2019). Another study by Yeung (1996) on the acute effects of exercise on mood state shows that on days when people exercise, they experience more positive interactions with friends and family. As early as 1996 Yeung wondered why, given that we know regular exercise is so beneficial, some 70% of us tend to be too lazy or busy to do it.

The lessons are clear. Exercise with your loved ones. It will help you get through the stresses of this strange time.

Chapter 12

Physical exercise
Ideas for indoor activities

In 1553, a Spanish doctor working in the Americas wrote one of the first exercise manuals. Dr Mendez wisely said that the best way to get busy people to exercise is to make it entertaining rather than give them pious advice they are likely to ignore. His patients were conquistadors and usually busy whipping Aztec slaves to mine gold and silver.

'*Mens sana in corpore sano*', a healthy mind in a healthy body, the Romans used to say. This chapter includes exercises you can make part of your daily life without becoming obsessive. Keeping a record of what you do is important, as isolation can play tricks with memory.

The British government allows going out for exercise but there is much we can do while inside, even in a small flat. Strength or resistance training is also vital for many reasons; besides the obvious muscle-building, it burns more calories and keeps bones strong, among other benefits. Squatting, arm raises and leg raises are good examples.

I intend to follow Mendez's advice and make the exercises entertaining. It's best to approach them with a sense of humour. There is proper psychological evidence that humour and laughing help you stay healthy. You'll have plenty to laugh about, as some of the exercises may seem daft at first.

My mother did the splits at 70

I have dedicated this book to my mother's memory. She often walked around her flat with a book on her head, and until she was in her 70s, she had excellent posture. Until the last years of her life, she did her gymnastic exercises every day for about 40 minutes. She could do the splits when she was 70.

My mother grew up in the late 1920s, when physical culture was popular in Europe. She had never hoped to be a ballet dancer or a gymnast. She trained as a lawyer. My father, also a lawyer, made fun of her obsession with physical fitness. I watched her with admiration when I was boy, but I had not the slightest intention of imitating her routines.

She didn't give up on me. When I was older she often nagged me to swim, run, play tennis, go to the gym.

"Later," I used to say, "when I've got time."

I never had time. Once I left school, I did no sports. The only time I did any strenuous exercise was the morning after I had gone to see a ballet based on Ravel's *Bolero*. The lead dancer swung and swivelled as Ravel's beat got faster and faster. The next day, by some coincidence, *Bolero* was on the radio. I got up and started gyrating as the astonishing dancer whose name I still remember – Jorge Lavelli – had done the night before.

I was about 34 years old then. I don't think I did anything like that for the next 16 years. I was ignoring a key fact: the human body was not designed to loll on the sofa or in bed. It has more than 600 muscles, which suggests it was made to exercise. Physical inactivity is the fourth leading cause of death globally, according to the World Health Organization in its briefing on Global Strategy on Diet, Physical Activity and Health published in 2010.

Is there any reason why you shouldn't dance a little every day in your living room? Try it. And reflect on this new maxim: dance and the world dances with you – slob and you'll soon slob alone.

Richard Asher, a well-known physician in the 1960s and 1970s, argued that laziness is bad for us. In his classic text, *Talking Sense About Medicine* (2015), he warned doctors of the dangers of keeping patients in bed, especially in a hospital. In an introduction to his book, his daughter, the actor Jane Asher, wrote: "none of us could put our head round his study door without being embroiled in some interesting thought he'd just had."

Asher provided a catalogue of ills and infections that would fester in bed. He was not, of course, warning of mere couch potatoing, but of 24-hour so-called bed rest, which seemed an ideal way to prepare a patient for the coffin. His ideas are relevant when we are isolated and, even if we are physically healthy, may be tempted to hole up in bed.

Going to bed, Asher argued in *Talking Sense About Medicine*, depressed many vital functions, including the respiratory system as well as the muscles. When our legs do not move, the venous blood "lacks the 'helpful squeeze from the muscles which normally speeds its flow. . . . The weight of the leg on the bed also compressed the calves and emptied the calf veins" (2015). He pointed out that 53% of patients who had been in bed a long time had thrombosis of the calf veins.

Asher was especially worried by 'foot drop', and woe betide the bedridden when they were finally let out of bed. They would hobble painfully on what weakened bones they had left. They also developed urinary infections, which led to kidney stones. On top of that, bed-confined patients often lost their appetite and started to suffer from heartburn, dyspepsia and constipation.

Asher's warning about the mental effects of staying in bed also apply to 'buttock idle'. I prefer the phrase to 'bone idle' because you slump on your buttocks. The patient, he wrote, in *Talking Sense About Medicine*, "loses the desire to get up and even resents any efforts to extract him from his supine stupor". Stupor was scientifically spot on. As soon as you sit down, electrical activity shuts off in the leg muscles. You can burn as little as one calorie an hour. Lipase, an enzyme in the legs that helps the breakdown of fat, plummets. After two hours of sitting, HDL (the so-called good cholesterol) levels drop by 20%. After 24 hours of sitting, insulin effectiveness drops 24% and the risk for diabetes rises. Sitting increases the risk of death up to 40%, according to Asher again.

But once you move it all changes for the better. Movement helps

- Lower blood pressure
- Improve regulation of blood sugar
- Lower resting heart rate
- Improve control of body fat
- Improve immune function
- Increase muscular strength and endurance
- Improve cardiorespiratory functioning
- Increase flexibility
- Improve joint health
- Improve mental functioning
- Create better dreams . . . well . . . quality of sleep

In their search for clarity out of many controversies, psychologists and doctors often go in for what is called 'meta-analysis', which means they review hundreds, even thousands, of studies, to sift out what we really know, what we can extrapolate – and what we should take with a pinch of salt.

Darren E. R. Warburton (2006), Crystal Whitney Nicol and Shannon S. D. Bredin of the School of Human Kinetics, University of British Columbia and the Healthy Heart Program of St Paul's Hospital Vancouver, BC, compared hundreds of such studies. Their conclusions should jolt you if you don't want to get going. Being physically inactive was the biggest 'modifiable risk factor'. You can't do anything about your genes, but you can do something about your couch potato tendencies and lessen your risk of succumbing to cardiovascular diseases, diabetes, cancer, osteoporosis and depression, which will delay your inevitable appointment with the undertakers.

To benefit from the physical and psychological effects of exercise, adults should do at least five 30-minute bouts of moderate to vigorous physical activity each week. A relatively small number of us actually achieve this, as low as 29% in some parts of the world (Hallal et al., 2012).

When we exercise, we increase our capillary blood supply to the cortex, from which new neurons and synapses grow, resulting in better learning and performance. Studies have found that, right across the adult age group, moderate exercise has many benefits. A meta analysis of 14 studies (covering over 230,000 participants) found those who run regularly have a 27% lower risk of all-cause mortality, a 30% lower risk of cardiovascular disease and a 23%

lower risk of cancer (Pedisic et al., 2020). They found even running just once a week could be beneficial.

High-intensity aerobic exercise (around 30 minutes of it) will facilitate better cognitive performance. Even acute, short-term bouts of resistance or moderate intensity exercise can improve cognitive performance and improve mood (Mandolesi et al., 2018).

Absorb the science. If you are isolated, do not let yourself mope and become lazy. Summon your inner sergeant major and encourage him or her to kick you into action. These exercises are for people indoors. Even if you have to stay inside you can still work out.

> Think of the positions in which you could start reading this book:
> Stand on one leg.
> Squat on your haunches.
> Do a classic ballet exercise like putting your leg up on a bar. You need to warm up first, but see how many you can manage: De-arabesque and return to a standing position.

If we were meant to lie like a rug, would evolution have given us such good legs? It isn't just celebs like George Clooney and the Duchess of Cambridge who have good legs – all legs are good. They just need action.

If you think it'll help, talk to your legs. I said humour is good, so I'll indulge in a little theatre of the absurd. My playlet stars me and my leg:

> Me: What have you been doing for the last 30 minutes?
> My Leg: Give me a break.
> Me: I don't want to break my leg. Just get up.
> My Leg: Next you'll be wanting a leg over.
> Me: Leave the jokes to brain. Your purpose in life is to shift your pins.

At the end of every day recall how much exercise you've taken and note that in a diary. You can then see if you are taking more exercise or just thinking about it. It takes discipline, but in isolation your memory may not be that reliable, so you need a record.

The head is an excellent place to start.

Balance the books

Put a book on your head. Best to start with a normal paperback, nothing too heavy.

Now start walking, trying to make sure the book does not fall off. You may find at first you can't do it, but keep trying. African and Indian women walk miles with jugs on their head and do it elegantly. An Italian woman in a deli told me her mother used to balance mortadella, a large barrel-shaped sausage, on her head. So surely you can manage to walk from one end of your living room to the other with just a James Bond paperback on your head.

The goals of the exercises that follow are to stay limber, to maintain good posture, to stretch, to keep the body flexible and to keep busy. Inactivity often leads to depression and asking, "Why is this happening to me?"

It isn't just happening to you or to me but to millions of us. Perspective is important. Feeling 'poor me' won't help you or those who have to deal with you.

Crumple every paper

Crumple a piece of paper and throw it on the floor. If you do not live alone, you need to explain to whoever you live with that you will be littering your abode with crumpled paper, but that there is a purpose to it. Crumpled envelopes, crumpled junk mail, crumpled anything you can pick up, are all important aids to fitness.

Children love making messes, so this new habit can help put you back in touch with your 2-year-old self who loved to spread chocolate, Legos and much else on the floor, driving the parents potty. If you have children, they'll love it. But tell them they can only do it after you have finished work.

If your significant others love you, they'll understand. It's not as if you're going to be taking an axe to your furniture.

Leave the crumpled paper on the floor and prepare for the next exercise.

Swing the leg

Stand with your legs apart. Swing your right arm to touch your left foot 25 times. Then swing your left arm to touch your right foot.

Isolation may bring out your inner masochist. Fight that. Throughout this, little rewards matter, so don't neglect them. Remember the 17th-century philosopher John Locke, who praised the Jewish habit of teaching small children the alphabet by using letters made from small biscuits. When a kid recognised a letter, he was allowed to eat it.

I often reward myself with a tomato juice and a handful of cashew nuts. Only you know what will feel like a good reward for you. It could be dark chocolate, a glass of cognac or another pint.

The ball exercise

In isolation you need to keep your reflexes sharp.

Find the largest room where you live and make sure that one wall is clear of pictures. You don't want a hole in your Picasso. My lawyers tell me to add that I take no responsibility for any damage you cause. The drinks industry says drink responsibly, so throw responsibly.

Find a tennis ball.

Stand about 6 to 7 feet away from the wall. Throw the ball as hard as you can against the wall. Catch it. Make it harder by throwing the ball at more than of an angle. If you drop the ball, squat to pick it up – and throw it again.

Sliding your hands down your knees

Sit on a chair and slide your hands down to your toes.

You can add the frill of putting a finger between each of your toes. Wiggle a finger between your toes. Keeping your toes flexible, and clean of fluff, is a good thing.

Squat for your brain

In a Horizon film on old age I made in 1981, I interviewed Bernard Isaacs, a professor of geriatric medicine at Birmingham University. He told me the way to avoid Alzheimer's was to squat. As often as you can. As you get older your balance deteriorates, Isaacs explained. He believed there was some connection between having a good sense of balance and the mind continuing to function well. He also believed in '*mens sana in corpore sano*'. He established a gait laboratory to work on balance and falls in old age. So squat.

I am sorry I did not insist that we do the interview squatting. Nor did I start squatting every day. But one domestic appliance has been designed to encourage the squat – the dishwasher.

> Pick up the plates, knives, spoons and forks from the table.
> Open the dishwasher.
> Squat and place one piece of crockery or cutlery in the dishwasher. Just one piece at a time.
> After you have put each one in, get up and return to your standing position.
> Repeat the squat and get up as you put in separately the spoons, the forks and each plate.
> Do it rhythmically. Squat – put item in dishwasher – rise – squat – put item in dishwasher – rise. It will help to listen to music as you do this.

When the dishwasher has finished, do the exercise in reverse. Pick up each item, rise, put it in its right place, squat, pick the next item up and carry on.

In the wash – bathrooms aren't just for ablutions

There is no reason why you shouldn't use your time in the bathroom for more than sluicing, as the great comic writer P.G. Wodehouse put it. His hero Bertie always had Jeeves run a bath for him. You probably won't have a butler to make sure the water is nice and hot but not too hot. Don't let your lack of domestic servants stop you.

Even the bathroom offers possibilities.

The arabesque while brushing your teeth

I was brushing my teeth in the bathroom when I suddenly thought how can I use the time I'm cleaning my teeth creatively. My unconscious ballet dancer self suddenly sparked.

I put my right leg up on the sink.

Then with my right hand, I touched the toes on my right foot 50 times while brushing my teeth. It's best to do this while you brush with an electric toothbrush.

Do the exercise as described above, putting one leg on the sink and touching your toes while brushing your teeth.

When I finished, I put my left leg up on the sink and touched the toes on my left foot. This was harder, but I still did 50.

This is a classic stretching exercise with an added refinement. You have to have a good enough sense of balance and coordination to work three limbs.

Your arm stretching to your toes.

Your leg up on the sink stretching your leg muscles.

Your other arm continuing to brush, which involves keeping pressure on the toothbrush.

Put your leg up on the basin and touch your toes while brushing your teeth. It makes you flexible and keeps teeth clean. Ideally count to 50 while doing this.

Two weeks into lockdown, Russian dancers posted videos of themselves dancing in their houses while they cleaned their kitchens and did housework. Some choreographer is bound to incorporate such scenes into a ballet.

If you feel like surprising your dentist, next time you have a filling, give him a demonstration of this exercise.

The car is an exercise machine too

In the touching film *The Karate Kid*, Mr Miyagi makes his student Daniel wax his car in an exercise known as 'wax on wax off'. Waxing on and waxing off builds up strength and flexibility. It's a perfect example of incorporating exercise into daily life. In the film, Mr Miyagi rewards Daniel eventually by giving him the car, and Daniel wins the karate competition against the bullies who have never waxed on or waxed off. The remake with Jackie Chan has the same waxing sequence.

The Karate Kid was a lovely story that appealed to children – and remembering how my mother nagged me to exercise, I'm glad to have some research that justified her nagging.

Physical activity significantly improves the way children behave, allowing them to co-operate better, decrease aggressiveness, take more responsibility and reduce antisocial behaviour. These all increase a child's ability to perform in an academic environment.

Schmidt and colleagues (2015) studied the impact of an acute bout of coordinated exercise on the attention of 90 primary school children and found that children paid more attention for up to 90 minutes after they finished physical exercise. Overall, the largest effects of acute bouts of physical activity occur 11–20 minutes after exercise and last only a brief time after children stop exercising.

At the start of the book I mentioned Tarzan, who loved action. There were no neuropsychologists roaming the jungle in his day, but I would bet that if there had been, they would have found he was buzzing with endorphins. In lockdown it's important to remember them. And also, don't forget to remove all the crumpled paper you have left on the floor from earlier on.

Chapter 13

Making the most of lockdown

Study something new

Being isolated gives us time to think, which can be a blessing or not. In our time-starved lives, we do not often get the kind of free time isolation forces on us. And that prompts basic questions:

> Do you see free time as an opportunity?
> Or does it just make you feel restless and depressed?

Shakespeare saw it as an opportunity. He wrote *King Lear* when he was quarantined during the Great Plague. Gwyneth Paltrow urges us to write a book, teach ourselves to code online and learn a language. Teen idol Harry Styles has said he's learning sign language *and* Italian.

Let's go with the Italian.

The movie *The Godfather* (1972) is seen as the fount of all wisdom by many people. In isolation we will need wisdom, but I prefer to turn to Churchill rather than to Don Corleone. Churchill suffered from the black dog, which I have argued in other books was not depression but mild bipolar disorder. At the start of his book *Painting as a Pastime*, Churchill comes close to describing depression himself: "Many remedies are suggested for the avoidance of worry and mental overstrain by persons who, over prolonged periods, have to bear exceptional responsibilities and discharge duties upon a very large scale." Travel, rest and exercise could help, he pointed out. He then quotes an unnamed American psychologist, who had said that worry "is a spasm of the emotion; the mind catches hold of something and will not let it go". Churchill continued that it was "useless to argue with the mind in this condition. The stronger the will, the more futile the task".

For Churchill, the crisis came in November 1915 when he had to resign as First Lord of the Admiralty after the disaster of the Gallipoli campaign. His loss of responsibility and power left him stunned. "Like a sea beast fished up from the depths, or a diver too suddenly hoisted, my veins threatened to burst from the fall in pressure. I had great anxiety and no means of relieving it." Reading was no escape; the remedy for Churchill's ills was to be found in painting: "To restore psychic equilibrium we should call into use those parts of the mind which direct both eye and hand."

The psychiatrist Viktor Frankl often recommended to his patients – even if they were dying – that they study something new. Learning is interesting and a distraction, he argued. It could help you park your complexes. Even fear of death. Patients could study Turkish, romantic Portuguese poetry or the history of cricket – anything they fancied.

Following Frankl's advice, and because years ago my sons and I visited the site of the original Olympics in Greece, I decided to look up a few details about them and share them. The old Olymbods (why not call them that) smeared themselves in olive oil often. The idea seems to have been to get as slippery as possible for wrestling contests.

Two other events struck me as eccentric and interesting. The first was running on the spot. This requires little explanation, though I am not sure how the winner was decided. The other event was the standing long jump. While running on the spot did not ever feature in the modern Olympics, the standing long jump did from 1896 to 1912.

Many of us have said if only I had the time, I'd like to study x or y. Now you may have the time. And if you can't think of x or y, there are the endless puzzles in newspapers, magazines, TV and the internet. Every day *The Times* carries its crossword so beloved of Colin Dexter's Inspector Morse, as well as the easier Quick Cryptic and the Times 2 Crossword for those who are anagram challenged. The paper also offers three Sudokus, the difficult, the fiendish and the super fiendish. Readers can also test their brains with three mental arithmetic puzzles as well as a Suko, a Polygon, the Train Tracks, a Lexica as well as a Codeword puzzle. You could spend three hours doing the lot before turning to the daily 15 general knowledge questions, which demand knowledge of anything and everything from historical hit records to the paintings of Rembrandt. The less highbrow *Evening Standard* offers nearly as many test-your-neurons games.

Learn Yiddish, Pidgin or Japanese

As I'm Jewish, I have toyed with brushing up my Yiddish, and since I managed to learn a few words of Japanese when I was there in the 1980s, I thought why not brush that up? It's a chance for everyone to toy with learning one of the world's languages. There are many basic books on how to start Japanese; *First Thousand Words in Japanese* is aimed at both adults and children. I have stressed the need to be playful, so I allow myself this fantasy. If you have children who are interested in dinosaurs, this may be the moment to help the children teach Japanese to the dinosaurs.

My reasons for suggesting Yiddish are more personal. Between the 17th and the end of the 19th centuries most Jews were not accountants, doctors or lawyers, but poor farmers and shopkeepers who lived in what was called the *shtetl*. They were often persecuted. Yiddish allowed them to talk freely among themselves without fear of reprisals.

So to lapse into Yiddish. Now is the time to get off your *tuchas* (backside) and start using your *keppe* (head)! These Yiddish words will come in handy to describe this pandemic *mishegas* (craziness).

1. Tsedrayte

adj. all mixed up, confused

Before the COVID-19 virus, *tsedrayte* meant you couldn't remember if you promised to meet a friend for lunch on Thursday or Friday. Now we don't know what day of the week it is. These days, just getting the mail makes us *tsedrayte*. Do we leave the letters on the floor for 24 hours? Do we wipe the package before we put it on the floor or wash our hands and then wipe the package? And what do we do after we open it?

2. Shpilkes

n. impatience, restlessness

Before the virus, when our young kids had 'ants in their pants', we'd tell them to go outside and play. Now, however, we have to mask them up first, and watch them carefully so they stay 2 metres from all the other kids.

3. Shlub

n. a slob; some who dresses sloppily

All this self-quarantining has made *shlubs* even *shlubbier*. I have argued elsewhere that we need to stay reasonably smart, brush our hair, shave (if male) and wash not just our hands so we unshlub. Don't just groom from the waist up for your Zoom conference calls.

4. Sekhel

n. common sense; good judgement

Our parents would nag us: "Have a little *sekhel*; look before you cross the road." Now the tables have turned, and we nag our parents: "Wash your hands. Wear a mask. You're *going* to the shops? You're old. Stay home!" And our kids? They have the computer *sekhel* we need: they've taught us how to complete the online school attendance form and how to limit our Facebook posts to 'friends only' so we don't embarrass them in front of the whole world!

5. Eyngeshparter

n. a stubborn person; someone who cannot be convinced with logic

These are the people who are protesting to end the shutdown before it's safe, ordering 'cures' on the internet and claiming the pandemic is all a hoax.

6. Ongeblozzen

adj. sulky, pouty; a sourpuss

Our kids used to get *ongeblozzen* when we said we couldn't go out for pizza. Now everyone's *ongeblozzen* because we spent all afternoon making dough from scratch . . . and we didn't have the right kind of cheese. "It tastes funny. It doesn't taste like Pizza Express. Why can't we go there?"

7. Tsuris

n. troubles and worries; problems

We can't help worrying when our sister tells us she had a suspicious mammogram or our son hints that someone bullied him in school. But these days, instead of worrying about illness *or* money *or* school *or* our family *or* the future, we're worried about *all* of it. *Tsuris* has gone from personal to universal.

8. Oy

int. (OY)

The most popular Yiddish expression, *oy* conveys dozens of emotions, from surprise, joy and relief to pain, fear and grief. Some optimists used to say that just groaning a good '*oy*' could make you feel better.

Avoid gurus

In *The Sunday Times* on 28 May, David Aaronovitch (2020) warned that plagues give gurus a boost. We long for solutions. I agree with him, but as I researched I found some interesting ideas developed by Rhi Wilmot (2020) of Bangor University.

She argues that while there are many uncontrollable elements of our current situation, we still have the capacity to do things that develop our skills, connect us socially and have a beneficial impact on other people. Going out for a simple bike ride does not just keep us fit but sets a good example for others (Wilmot, 2020):

> This promotes 'meaning salience' – the extent to which we are aware of exactly what it is that makes our life meaningful. Levels of meaning salience can vary from day-to-day, but higher amounts boost our

psychological wellbeing, and serve as a link between an abstract conception of the future, and what we do today.

She argues lockdown can be an opening up as it "offers us time and space for introspection, and a chance to build greater self-awareness than ever before". She refers to 'post-traumatic growth', which I mentioned in discussing how some of those held hostage on the trains in Holland in 1977 felt the trauma changed their lives for the better. Will lockdown do the same, changing how we perceive the world and our place in it?

Wilmot is an optimist and says, "perhaps the present uncertainty will give rise to new forms of meaning. When we emerge from the chrysalis of lockdown, this resource will help us greet the world with purpose."

But that will only happen if we keep our minds active in the pandemic.

Chapter 14

The experiment

What the pandemic has taught us so far about human nature

Very occasionally a real-life event may present a great research opportunity. My favourite example was recorded in *When Prophecy Fails* (Festinger et al., 1956). A small group of believers had concluded the world would end at a particular time and that everyone would be killed, apart from a small group of believers. Three psychologists joined the group, pretending they shared the belief. They noted how people reacted first in the days, then hours, then minutes before the end of the world and then how they responded when the world did not end and they were not whisked off to safety in outer space. To the surprise of the psychologists, the believers did not lose their faith but intensified their efforts to recruit new members. It remains a powerful real-life experiment.

The virus and lockdowns are a worldwide phenomenon and also an experiment. We have to deal with it. It will take time to see and study the effects, but there is some value in first impressions and questions. I concentrate first on the psychological questions. The answers offered are very preliminary.

Who copes well with isolation – and who suffers?

In May the Resolution Foundation (2020) revealed that young people in work were being disproportionately hit by unemployment: a third of 18- to 24-year-olds in work had lost their jobs, compared with one in six adults. The Institute for Fiscal Studies has found that mothers are 23% more likely than fathers to have lost their jobs (temporarily or permanently) during the current crisis, 47% more likely than fathers to have permanently lost their job or quit and 14% more likely to have been furloughed.

What impact has there been on domestic violence?

Over three months it will be possible to see if rates of homicide, suicide and serious violence have changed. Childcare charities report they have been contacted more than usual. The increase in domestic violence has been looked at in Chapter 6.

To what extent have people in the UK and other countries complied with restrictions imposed by their governments?

The British have complied with the rules more than expected, but they have also made increasing fun of the government, as *The Times'* Celebrity Watch concluded on 28 May.

I leave three questions unanswered for now.

Do people feel they have changed as a result of the isolation?
How has this affected faith in the government given the obvious errors made in the UK at the start of the crisis?
Do people think this will go on for ever and indeed change the world forever?

All these questions need data and analysis (and the data changes all the time).

In terms of social psychology, the epidemic has forced people to accept more intrusion into their lives. Track, trace and isolate helped countries like South Korea, Germany and Taiwan restrict the spread of the virus early on. Britain introduced track and trace extremely late, for a variety of unflattering reasons. Some states in the United States have deployed it but others have not. There continues to be resistance there, where it seems that half the population suspects government agencies of trying to control their lives in ways that violate the Constitution. *Wired's* Emma Grey Ellis (2020) describes this as "a modern permutation of an identity crisis with roots very deep in America's individualist history".

The virus should motivate political psychologists, as it allows them to investigate one fundamental question: How threatened do you have to be before you compromise on freedom?

Americans who hate the lockdown often hark back to the original 1773 Boston Tea Party. Infuriated by the tax demands of George III, Bostonians threw tea chests off the ships into the harbour. Their violence helped spark the American Revolution – and a legacy of this is that Americans are very suspicious of big government and government interference.

The American reaction recently has not been pretty, however. Anti-lockdown activists have worn swastikas in Michigan, while there has been a huge increase in gun sales all over the United States. It sounds like an exam question: "The virus breeds fear and intolerance. Discuss."

Two of the world's least-tolerant politicians – President Trump and Brazilian Jair Bolsonaro – feel coronavirus is almost a hoax and oppose the strict lockdown measures many of their state governors have implemented. "Unemployment, hunger and misery will be the future of those who support the tyranny of total isolation," Bolsonaro recently tweeted. He also joined anti-lockdown protestors outside his offices in Brasilia, the nation's capital. "Above all [they] want freedom, they want democracy, they want respect," Bolsonaro recently said. And they want work.

The number of deaths in both countries has been great – 142,595 in the United States and 81,487 in Brazil at the time of writing, according to the COVID-19 Dashboard of the Center for Systems Science and Engineering at Johns Hopkins University. But as *When Prophecy Fails* might predict, the number of deaths has not stopped those who do not believe in the virus from refusing to change their attitudes or behaviour. The irrationality of some responses is clearest in Germany. Its government made social distancing work, used track and trace and kept the number of confirmed deaths relatively low. Activists have still protested against lockdown measures every Saturday – and each week, the demonstrations attract a more and more extreme audience.

Psychologists have the opportunity to study the huge differences between those who want government to provide a sense of the old normal and those who want to mitigate COVID-19's lethal risks. One side stresses freedom, the other health. There will probably be a vocal group protesting against any measures, and that is bound to make any nation's coronavirus recovery harder, according to Thomas Carothers and David Wong (2020) of the Carnegie Endowment for International Peace in Washington, DC.

It was generally expected there would be some resistance in Britain to the lockdown restrictions, but they have, on the whole, been accepted. The revelation that Dominic Cummings broke the rules he helped write by driving north has had an effect on public opinion. Opinion polls find support for the government fell by 8% in the week after his press conference in the Downing Street Rose Garden.

Psychologists may also contribute to studying the inequality of deaths. According to the figures produced by the government at its daily briefings, people from ethnic minority backgrounds constitute 14% of the population but account for 34% of critically ill COVID-19 patients and a similar percentage of all COVID-19 cases. These patterns are not unique to the UK – in Chicago, black people constitute 30% of the population but account for 72% of deaths from the virus.

On 29 July the British government announced a series of studies to examine the issues, including one theory that those from BAME (black, Asian and minority ethnic) backgrounds suffer more from cardiovascular disorders and diabetes, which can reduce people's ability to recover from COVID-19. One study will focus on occupations. Men and women from BAME backgrounds constitute a disproportionately high number of key frontline workers like public transport drivers, cleaners, Band 5 nurses and carers, according to a Office for National Statistics (2020) report.

It is not just those with a BAME background who are most at risk. Meredith Wadman (2020) has reported in *Science* that sex hormones may explain why men suffer more. In January 2020, one of the first papers on the virus reported that in Wuhan three out of every four hospitalised patients were male. More data from around the world have since confirmed that men face a greater risk of severe illness and death from COVID-19 than women.

Androgens – male hormones such as testosterone – appear to improve the virus' ability to get inside cells. Research from Spain suggests that a disproportionate number of men with male pattern baldness – which is linked to a powerful androgen – end up in hospitals with COVID-19. Testing drugs that block androgens' effects and deploying them early is a possible way of slowing the virus and buying time for the immune system to act. Two small studies have reported that men with male pattern baldness are overrepresented among hospitalised COVID-19 patients. An April 2020 study of 41 Spanish men hospitalised for COVID-19 found that 71% had male pattern baldness; the background rate in white men is estimated at 31% to 53% (Young Workers in the Coronavirus Crisis, 2020). The second study reported in the *Daily Mail* online by Vanessa Chalmers found that 79% of 122 men in three Madrid hospitals with COVID-19 had male pattern baldness.

Christina Jamieson (Wadman, 2020) of the University of California (UC), San Diego, recalls that she was in a Zoom meeting discussing how to link her prostate cancer research to COVID-19 when her sister, also a UC San Diego scientist, sent her a one-word text. It read: "TMPRSS2." The virus that causes COVID-19 relies in part on TMPRSS2, an enzyme that smooths the path for the virus to fuse with the host cell's membrane and get inside the cell.

Human competitiveness still thrives. The race to find a cure or vaccine sometimes seems like the race in 1953 to reach the summit of Everest. Blood or plasma from recovered patients has been tried as a therapy since at least the Spanish flu of 1918; reports from that pandemic suggest it helped. It has also been used to fight measles, severe acute respiratory syndrome and lesser-known diseases such as Argentine haemorrhagic fever. "I think that it has a high likelihood [of working] based on history," says Arturo Casadevall of Johns Hopkins University (Casadevall and Pirofski, 2020). He has followed up on this and on 13 March 2020, he published what he considers "maybe the most important paper" of his long career. In the *Journal of Clinical Investigation* (2020), he and Liise-anne Pirofski of Albert Einstein College of Medicine argued that one effective treatment might already be at hand: the blood plasma of people who have recovered from the disease, rich in antibodies against the virus. The risks are comparatively low. "We recommend that institutions . . . begin preparations as soon as possible," they wrote and added "Time is of the essence" (Casadevall and Pirofski, 2020).

Ten weeks later, more than 16,000 patients in US hospitals had received the experimental therapy and the hope that it works could soon give way to evidence. A study of patients treated at Mount Sinai Hospital in New York City, published as a preprint on 22 May, offers hints it may, as do other small studies elsewhere. But to be sure, randomised controlled clinical trials (RCTs) will be needed.

We have to prepare for what may be a very changed world – or what may be a world that has just had a bad scare and will return to normal, more or less. I am a psychologist, not a futurologist, but psychological studies suggest futurologists are not wizards. Psychiatrists cannot even predict which of their patients, when released from secure hospitals like Broadmoor, will cope and which will commit dangerous acts. So what follows is speculation.

After the Black Death, which killed a quarter of the world's population, the world did change, but slowly. The feudal system died; the Renaissance changed culture and, at the same time, Columbus 'discovered' America. It would be astonishing if this virus (which will kill far fewer people, based on even the worst predictions) provokes such profound changes.

But there will be changes – and changes we cannot predict. That must make us anxious, but it is an intriguing thought. Some guesses follow.

We will travel less, having discovered the wonders of Zoom and video conferencing – although negotiators on the Brexit deal insist it is much harder to negotiate when you cannot have a cup of coffee with your 'partners' at the end of a session. Psychologists should compare body language in the flesh with body language in remote dealings.

Shopping will change drastically as shops have to allow fewer people in and insist they move through the shop methodically and not double back to see if they really do want to buy that item. Shops are used to a small number of awkward customers. What do they do with the customer who just will not play by the new rules? And the idiot who does not hand sanitise?

I also am intrigued by the use of masks and how that will affect the perception of speech and body language. Good subjects to study.

As I have outlined in small steps as the data comes in, we are learning more about what isolation, and isolation in small groups, tells us about the nature of human nature. The different views are best illustrated perhaps by a novelist and a sea captain.

William Golding wrote the novel *Lord of the Flies*, which became a seminal text, in 1951. In it, a group of middle-school-age boys become stranded on an island without adult supervision and their community descends into chaos. The Romans said '*homo hominis lupus*' – man is a wolf to other men – and Golding's dark book seemed to offer proof of that. But 15 years later, in the real world, an event cast doubt on how universal Golding's vision was.

In 1966, Captain Peter Warner was sailing by a small uninhabited island named Ata – at least it was supposed to be uninhabited. But Peter noticed something odd. Peering through his binoculars, he saw burned patches on the green cliffs. "In the tropics it's unusual for fires to start spontaneously," he told us, a half century later (Warner, 2020). Then he saw a boy. Naked. Hair down to his shoulders. This wild creature leaped from the cliffside and plunged into the water. Suddenly more boys followed, screaming at the top of their lungs. It did not take long for the first boy to reach the boat. "My name is Stephen," he cried in perfect English. "There are six of us and we reckon we've been here 15 months."

The boys, once aboard, claimed they were students at a boarding school in Nuku'alofa, the Tongan capital. Sick of school meals, they had decided to take a fishing boat out one day, only to get caught in a storm. Likely story, Peter thought. Using his two-way radio, he called in to Nukuʻalofa. "I've got six kids here", he told the operator. "Stand by", came the response. Twenty minutes ticked by. (As Peter tells this part of the story, he gets a little misty-eyed.) Finally, a very tearful operator came on the radio and said: "You found them! These boys have been given up for dead. Funerals have been held. If it's them, this is a miracle!" The boys' story was quite different than the one in *Lord of the Flies*.

This book started out personal, so I should end it by noting what I have learned in isolation.

I do not think I have been changed fundamentally by 10 days in isolation; 800 days would be different, perhaps.

I have become a bit more patient.

I have stayed in touch with old friends if only by phone.

I have lost weight because I have been eating less. None of the mounds of pasta that I used to consume.

I have smoked far less, even though my cigar merchant, Smokers Paradise, mails me cigars.

I have worried more about my son and his mother. Sane anxiety is a sign of love.

I have not drunk more than usual.

I have not taken a cab.

I worry about money, as my Airbnb sideline has collapsed along with the hospitality industry.

I have not been able to study something new because I have been writing this book. It has made me think, of course, but I no longer have unrealistic ambitions. At least I do not think this book will change the world.

As I have been sleeping badly, I have written some of it at 3 a.m. So isolation has not made me less work-obsessed.

I hope readers will find this book useful and timely. It is safe to predict the pandemic will lead to many more books and studies as we try to understand what countries did wrong and learn the lessons. The most sobering statistic is that 722,000 people had died of the virus by 17 August 2020, according to the COVID-19 Dashboard by the Center for Systems Science and Engineering at Johns Hopkins University. Many of these deaths could have been prevented if we had been prepared and learned the lessons of previous pandemics. That, on the basis of past history, will need us to be tough with ourselves. As this book goes to press late August, 2020, there is no sign that the world is managing to contain the virus. Vladimir Putin has announced that just as Russia was the first to launch Sputnik, it is now the first to have produced a vaccine. The world remains sceptical. Yet we must stay hopeful.

Select bibliography

Introduction

The American Philosophical Society, The Salvador E. Luria Papers Mss.Ms.Coll.39 1923–1992.

Ao, Bethany (2020) More People on Antidepressants, Anti Anxiety Medications during Pandemic. *MedicalXpress*. Accessed on 28 April from https://medicalxpress.com/news/2020-04-people-antidepressants-antianxiety-medications-pandemic.html

Aware, Association of Women for Action and Research Singapore (30 June 2020) AWARE's Submission to the United Nations Special Rapporteur.

Bauwens, M., Compernolle, S., Stavrakou, T., Müller, J.-F., van Gent, J., Eskes, H., et al. (2020). Impact of Coronavirus Outbreak on NO_2 Pollution Assessed Using TROPOMI and OMI Observations. *Geophysical Research Letters*, 47, e(2020)GL087978.

Bureau of Labour. (2020) *Statistics News Release*. https://www.bls.gov/news.release/pdf/empsit.pdf

Burroughs, Edgar Rice (1916) *The Beasts of Tarzan*. A. C. McClurg, Chicago.

Gecewicz, Claire (2020) *Few Americans Say Their House of Worship Is Open, But a Quarter Say Their Faith Has Grown Amid Pandemic Pew Research Centre Factank*. Accessed on 30 April from https://www.pewresearch.org/fact-tank/2020/04/30/few-americans-say-their-house-of-worship-is-open-but-a-quarter-say-their-religious-faith-has-grown-amid-pandemic

Hall, Stanley G. (1907) *Youth: Its Education, Regimen, and Hygiene*. D Appleton and Co, New York.

Johnson, Boris (3 April 2020) Letter from 10 Downing Street.

Lipuma, L. (11 May 2020) COVID 19 Lockdowns Significantly Impacting Global Air Quality. *Advancing Earth and Space Sciences*.

Luria, Salvador (1959) *The Bacterial Protoplasm*. American Philosophical Society Library, Philadelphia.

McCarthy, Todd (12 March 1995) Review of Outbreak. *Variety*.

Sambhi, Sonia (3 April 2020) Covid-19 and the Increase in Domestic Violence in Asia Pacific Eco-business. *Asian News Website*.

Sartre, Jean Paul (2019) *Huis Clos Gallimard*. Paris.

Scott, Sophie (2020) Can We Make Jokes about Coronavirus? *The Psychologist* March, 15.

The Trussel Trust End of Year Stats (2019) https://www.trusselltrust.org/news-and-blog/latest d-year-stats/

Chapter 1

Ascher, L.M., and Turner, R.M. (1979) Paradoxical Intention and Insomnia: An Experimental Investigation. *Behaviour Research and Therapy*, 17(4), 408–411.

Bateson, Gregory, Jackson, Don D., Haley, Jay, and Weakland, John (1956) *Toward a Theory of Schizophrenia*. John Wiley & Sons, Ltd., Chichester.

Bertero, Alice, Feyen, Paul Luc Caroline, Zurita, Hector, and Apicella, Alfonso Junior (23 October 2019) A Non-Canonical Cortico-Amygdala Inhibitory Loop. *Journal of Neuroscience*, 39(43), 8424–8438.

Espie, C.A., Lindsay, W.R., Brooks, D.N., Hood, E.M., and Turvey, T. (1989) A Controlled Comparative Investigation of Psychological Treatments for Chronic Sleep-onset Insomnia. *Behaviour Research and Therapy*, 27(1), 79–88.

Freud, S. (1953) *The Standard Edition of the Complete Psychological Works of Sigmund Freud, Volume VII (1901-1905): A Case of Hysteria, Three Essays on Sexuality and Other Works*, 123–246. Hogarth Press, London.

Jackson, Craig (17 March 2020) Coronavirus and Obsessive-type Conditions. *The Psychologist*.

Janes, Laura (9 March 2019) *Legal Director for the Howard League for Penal Reform's Complaint to the Prisons and Probation Ombudsman*, quoted in Youth Prison Put Inmates in Solitary Confinement for Up to 23 Hours a Day. *The Guardian*.

Lacks, P., Bertelson, A.D., Gans, L., and Kunkel, J. (1983) The Effectiveness of Three Behavioral Treatments for the Different Degrees of Sleep Onset Insomnia. *Behavior Therapy*, 14(5), 593–605.

Position Statement: Solitary Confinement (Isolation) (2016). *Journal of Correctional Health Care*, 22(3), 257–263.

Thomas, Virginia, and Azmitia, Margarita (2019) Motivation Matters: Development and Validation of the Motivation for Solitude Scale–Short Form (MSS-SF). *Journal of Adolescence*, 70, 33–42.

Turner, Ralph M., and Ascher, Michael L. (1982) Therapist Factor in the Treatment of Insomnia. *Behaviour Research and Therapy*, 20(1), 33–40.

Twose, Gabe (2016) *Solitary Confinement of Juvenile Offenders*. The American Psychological Association, APA Public Interest Government Relations Office Statement.

University College (2020) *Virus Watch University College*. website contact j.hawkes@uc.ac.uk.

Chapter 2

American Psychological Association (2016) *Solitary Confinement of Juvenile Offenders; Position Statement*.

Bamford, Thomas (12 September 2019) The Independent Monitoring Board (IMB) Have Released Their Damning Verdict on the Situation at HMP YOI Aylesbury. *The Bucks Herald*.

Brooks, Samantha, Webster, Becca, Smith, Louise, Woodland, Lisa, Wessely, Simon, Greenberg, Neil, and Rubin, James (26 February 2020) The Psychological Impact of Quarantine and How to Reduce It: Rapid Review of the Evidence. *The Lancet*, 395(10227), 912–920.

Cacioppo, J.T., and Cacioppo, S. (2018) The Growing Problem of Loneliness. *The Lancet*, 391(10119), 426.

Camp Camille, George, and Resnik, Judith (November 2016) *Aiming to Reduce Time-In-Cell: Reports from Correctional Systems on the Numbers of Prisoners in Restricted Housing and on the Potential of Policy Changes to Bring About Reforms*. Association of State Correctional Administrators, The Arthur Liman Public Interest Program, Yale Law School.

Clancy, Tom (1990) *The Hunt for Red October*. Harper Collins, London.

Independent Monitoring Board (August 2019) Annual Report of the Independent Monitoring Board at HM YOI Aylesbury for the Reporting Year 1st July 2018 to 18th March 2019.

Lobel, J., and Akil, Huda (2018) Law & Neuroscience: The Case of Solitary Confinement. *The American Academy of Arts & Sciences*, 147(4), 61–75.

Maitland, Sara (2009) *A Book of Silence*. Granta, London.

Sherwood, Harriet (9 March 2019) Youth Prison Put Inmates in Solitary Confinement for Up to 23 Hours a Day. *The Guardian*.

Smith, Dana G. (9 November 2018) On Neuroscientists Make a Case Against Solitary Confinement. *Scientific American*.

Smith, Nathan and Barrett, Emma (18 March 2020) Coping with Life in Isolation and Confinement During the Covid-19 Pandemic. *The Psychologist*.

Thomas, Virginia, and Azmitia, Margarita (2019) Motivation Matters: Development and Validation of the Motivation for Solitude Scale–Short Form (MSS-SF). *Journal of Adolescence*, 70, 32–43.

Travis, Jeremy, Western, Bruce, and Redburn, Steve, editors (2014) *The Growth of Incarceration in the United States, Exploring Causes and Consequences of High Rates of Incarceration, Committee on Law and Justice, Division of Behavioral and Social Sciences and Education.* National Research Council of the National Academies, Washington, DC.

Chapter 3

Bridge, Mark (4 June 2020) Isaac Newton's Plague Cure Fell Far From the Tree. *The Times*.

Camus, Albert (1947) *The Plague*. Gallimard, French, 1948 (Hamish Hamilton, English).

Camus, Albert, and Malraux, André (2016) *Albert Camus, André Malraux, Correspondance 1941–1959*. Gallimard, Paris.

Defoe, Daniel (1841) *A Journal of the Plague year in the Works: With a Memoir of His Life and Writings*. Clements, London.

di Coppo, Stefani, Cited in Benedictow, Ole Jørgen (2008) *The Black Death, 1346–1353: The Complete History*. Boydell Press, Woodbridge, Suffolk, and Rochester, NY.

Freeman, D., Waite, F., Rosebrock, L., Petit, A., Causier, C., East, A., and Lambe, S. (2020). Coronavirus Conspiracy Beliefs, Mistrust, and Compliance with Government Guidelines in England. *Psychological Medicine*, 1–13.

Spinney, L. (2018) *Pale Rider*. Vintage, New York.

Telegraph Reporters (3 June 2020) Divorce Inquiries up by 42pc Since Coronavirus Lockdown. *The Daily Telegraph*.

Chapter 4

Bake, B., Larsson, P., Ljungkvist, G., Ljungström, E., and Olin, A-C. (2019) Exhaled Particles and Small Airways. *Respiratory Research*, 20(8). Published online January 11. doi: 10.1186/s12931-019-0970-9

Buranyi, Stephen (1 May 2020) Inside Germany's Covid-19 Testing Masterclass. *Prospect Magazine*.

Burn-Murdoch, John, and Giles, Chris (28 May 2020) UK Suffers Second-highest Death Rate from Coronavirus. *Financial Times*.

CDC (2020) *Preliminary Report on Excess Deaths, Morbidity and Mortality*. CDC, Atlanta.

Camus, Albert (1947) *The Plague*. Gallimard, French, 1948 (Hamish Hamilton, English).

Camus, Albert, and Malraux, André (2016) *Albert Camus, André Malraux, Correspondance 1941–1959*. Gallimard, Paris, 152, 42.

Cho, Sun Young, Kang, Ji-Man, Ha, Young Eun, Park, Ga Eun, Lee, Ji Yeon, Ko, Jae-Hoon, et al. (3 September 2016) MERS-CoV Outbreak Following a Single Patient Exposure in an Emergency Room in South Korea: An Epidemiological Outbreak Study. *The Lancet*, 388(10048), 994–1001.

Day, M. (11 May 2020) Concerns About Social Care's Ability to Cope with a Pandemic Were Raised Two Years Ago. *BMJ*, 369, m1879. https://doi.org/10.1136/bmj.m1879.

Defoe, Daniel (1841) *A Journal of the Plague Year in the Works: With a Memoir of His Life and Writings*. Clements, London.

Dixon, F. Norman (1976) *On the Psychology of Military Incompetence*. Basic Books, New York.

Gupta, S. (7 May 2020) Why America's Social Distancing Efforts Have Had 'Painfully Slow' Results. *CNN*.

Hamner, L., Dubbel, P., Capron, I., et al. (March 2020). High SARS-CoV-2 Attack Rate Following Exposure at a Choir Practice – Skagit County, Washington. *Morbidity and Mortality Weekly Report*, 69, 606–610.

Kenber, Billy (21 May 2020) Trackers Complain of 'Chaotic' Training. *The Times*.

Kupferschmidt, Kai (19 May 2020) Why Do Some COVID-19 Patients Infect Many Others, Whereas Most Don't Spread the Virus at All? *Science*.

Kurcharski, Adam (2020) *The Rules of Contagion*. Wellcome, London.

Leclerc, Quentin, Fuller, Naomi, and Knight, Lisa (5 June 2020) CMMID COVID-19 Working Group, Funk, Sebastian, Knight, Gwenan. What Settings Have Been Linked to SARS-CoV-2 Transmission Clusters? *Wellcome Open Research*, 5, 83.

Lloyd-Smith, J., Kopp, P., Schreiber, S., and Getz, W.S. (2005) Superspreading and the Effect of Individual Variation on Disease Emergence. *Nature*, 438, 355–359.

MedicalXpress (30 June 2020).

Megerian, Chris (6 May 2020) Trump Calls Americans 'Warriors' in Fight to Open the Economy. *Los Angeles Times*.

Normile, D (2020) *Coronavirus Cases Have Dropped Sharply in South Korea. Science*.

Park, Hye, Park, Wan, Lee, So, Kim, Jeong-Lan, Lee, Jung, Lee, Haewoo, and Shin, Hyoung-Shik (2020) Posttraumatic Stress Disorder and Depression of Survivors 12 Months after the Outbreak of Middle East Respiratory Syndrome in South Korea. *BMC Public Health*, 20. https://doi.org/10.1186/s12889-020-08726-1.

Pegg, David, Booth, Robert, and Conn, David (7 May 2020) Revealed: The Secret Report that Gave Ministers Warning of Care Home Coronavirus Crisis. *The Guardian*.

Rayner, Vic (20 March 2020) UK Government Must Recognise Care Workers Are on the Coronavirus Frontline Too. *The Guardian*.

Stedman, Alex, and Donnelly, Matt (11 March 2020) Tom Hanks, Rita Wilson Test Positive for Coronavirus. *Variety*.

Thompson, Derek (22 May 2020) Derek Social Distancing Is Not Enough. *The Atlantic*.

US Centre for Disease Control (12 May 2020) Press Release. Atlanta.

Chapter 5

Comfort, Alex (1972) *The Joy of Sex*. Crown Publishing Group, New York.

Dicks, Jo (2018) *High Intensity Intercourse Training*. Pop Press, Nottingham.

Donne, J. (2012) *Collected Works*. Penguin Classics, London.

Lucchessi, E. (3 January 2019) The Unbearable Heaviness of Clutter. *New York Times*.

Stapley, Leslie, and Murdock, Nancy (2020) Leisure in Romantic Relationships: An Avenue for Differentiation of Self. *Personal Relationships*, 27. https://doi.org/10.1111/pere.12310.

Chapter 6

Asahi Shimbun (19 February 2019) 61% Think Abe Inadequately Handles Labor Survey Scandal.

Ashton, Kathryn, Bellis, Mark, Winstock, Adam, Hughes, Karen, and Davies, Alisha (2017) Do Emotions Related to Alcohol Consumption Differ by Alcohol Type? An International Cross-sectional Survey of Emotions Associated with Alcohol Consumption and Influence on Drink Choice in Different Settings. *BMJ Open*, 7(10), e016089. https://doi.org/10.1136/bmjopen-2017-016089

Bangkok Post (14 January 2016) Japan Lawmaker Says 'Comfort Women' Were 'Prostitutes'.

Batty, David (3 May 2020) Coronavirus Crisis Could Increase Users' Drug Habits – Report. *The Guardian*.

Bryant, Peter (1982) *Piaget Issues and Experiments*. British Psychological Society Books, Leicester.

Dixon, Norman F. (1976) *On the Psychology of Military Incompetence*. Random House, London.

Geiger, Ben, and Mackerron, George (2016) Can Alcohol Make You Happy? A Subjective Wellbeing Approach. *Social Science & Medicine*, 156.

Gilchrist, Gail, Dennis, Fay, Radcliffe, Polly, Henderson, Juliet, Howard, Louise M., Gadd, David (2019) The Interplay Between Substance Use and Intimate Partner Violence Perpetration: A Meta-ethnography. *International Journal of Drug Policy*, 65, 8–23.

Goleman, Daniel (1995) *Emotional Intelligence*. Bantam Books, New York.

Grierson, Jamie (15 April 2020) Domestic Abuse Killings 'More Than Double' Amid Covid-19 Lockdown. *The Guardian*.

Hester, M. (6 April 2020) Quoted in Locked Down, and More Vulnerable to Abuse. *The New York Times*.

House of Commons Home Affairs Committee (24 April 2020) *Home Office Preparedness for Covid-19 (Coronavirus): Domestic Abuse and Risks of Harm Within the Home Second Report of Session 2019–21*. London.

Hughes, M. (1978) Selecting Pictures of Another Person's View. *British Journal of Educational Psychology*, 48, 210–219.

Jeong, Hyunsuk, Woo Yim, Hyeon, Song, Yeong-Jun, Ki, Moran, Min, Jung-Ah, Cho, Juhee, and Chae, Jeong-Ho (2016) Mental Health Status of People Isolated Due to Middle East Respiratory Syndrome. *Epidemiology and Health*, 38, e2016048.

Kupferschmidt, Kai (19 May 2020) Why Do Some COVID-19 Patients Infect Many Others, Whereas Most Don't Spread the Virus at All? *Science*.

LAPD, Official Site of the Los Angeles Police Department Domestic Violence: Reasons Why Battered Victims Stay with the Batterers. http://lapdonline.org/get_informed/content_basic_view/8877

Leclerc, Q.J., Fuller, N.M., Knight, L.E., Funk, S., and Knight, G.M. (2020). COVID19 Settings of Transmission – Collected Reports Database [Data Collection]. *Figshare*. https://doi.org/10.6084/m9.figshare.12173343.v3

Lloyd-Smith, J.O., Schreiber, S.J., Kopp, P.E., and Getz, W.M. (2005) Superspreading and the Effect of Individual Variation on Disease Emergence. *Nature*, 438(7066), 355–359.

NHS Digital (2020) *Statistics on Alcohol*. England.

Payne, Leon (1985) *A Study of Emotion: Developing Emotional Intelligence; Self-Integration; Relating to Fear, Pain and Desire*. Dissertation, The Union for Experimenting Colleges and Universities.

Saxbe, D.E., & Repetti, R. (2010). No Place Like Home: Home Tours Correlate With Daily Patterns of Mood and Cortisol. *Personality and Social Psychology Bulletin*, 36(1), 71–81. https://doi.org/10.1177/0146167209352864

Shakespeare, Stephan (2020) How Are British Drinking Habits Shifting Under Lockdown? *YouGov* blog post. https://yougov.co.uk/topics/food/articles-reports/2020/04/08/how-are-british-drinking-habits-shifting-under-loc

Snugs, Tania (24 April 2020) Coronavirus: 4,000 Domestic Abuse Arrests in London in Just Six Weeks, Police Say. *Sky News.*

Taub, Amanda (6 April 2020) A New Covid-19 Crisis: Domestic Abuse Rises Worldwide. *The New York Times.*

UK Government Press Release (2020) *Emergency Funding to Support Most Vulnerable in Society During Pandemic.* https://www.gov.uk/government/news/emergency-funding-to-support-most-vulnerable-in-society-during-pandemic

Winstock, A.R., Davies, E.L., Gichrist, G., Zhuparris, A., Ferris, J.A., Maier, L.J., and Barratt, M.J. (2020) *Global Drug Survey Special Edition on Covid-19 Global Interim Report.* https://www.globaldrugsurvey.com/wp-content/themes/globaldrugsurvey/assets/GDS_COVID-19-GLOBAL_Interim_Report-2020.pdf

World Health Organization (2004) *Intimate Partner Violence and Alcohol.* Briefing. World Health Organization, Geneva.

You Gov Polls (17 April 2020) *Are You Drinking More or Less Alcohol Than You Normally Would?*

Chapter 7

Baird, Sarah, Friedman, Jed, and Schady, Norbert (2011) Aggregate Income Shocks and Infant Mortality in the Developing World. *The Review of Economics and Statistics,* 93(3), 847–856.

Cohen, D. (9 September 1971) Interview with John Bowlby. *New Scientist.*

Cohen, D. (2018) *Great Psychologists as Parents: Interview with Sir Richard Bowlby.* Routledge, London.

Cox, R.S. (6 April 2020) Experts Say Kids Need Help Expressing Their Feelings about the Pandemic. *CBC Radio.*

Fisher, Naoimi (3 April 2020) School's Really Out. *The Psychologist.*

Fothergill, Alice, and Peek, Lori (2015) *Children of Katrina.* University of Texas Press, Austin.

Gaulkin, Thomas (26 March 2020) Kids Are Drawing Pictures of the New Coronavirus. That's a Good Thing. *Bulletin of the Atomic Scientists.*

Gerwirtz, Abigail (2020) *When the World Feels Like a Scary Place: Essential Conversations for Anxious Parents and Worried Kids.* Workman Publishing, New York.

Goldberg, Joel (30 April 2020) Children of the Pandemic: How Will Kids Be Shaped by the Coronavirus Crisis? *Science Magazine.*

Goodman, S.H., and Garber, J. (2017) Evidence-Based Interventions for Depressed Mothers and Their Young Children. *Child Development,* 88(2), 368–377.

Guterres, A. (16 April 2020) The Impact of COVID 19 Pandemic on Children Statement.

Ippen, G., and Lieberman, A.F. (2019) *A Guide for Conducting Relationship Based Trauma Interventions.* Unpublished Manuscript.

Leong, Victoria, Santamaria, Lorena, Noreika, Valdas, Georgieva, Stanimira, Clackson, Kaili, and Wass, Sam (February 2020) Emotional Valence Modulates the Topology of the Parent-infant Inter-brain Network. *NeuroImage,* 207.

Luthar, Suniya, and Eisenberg, Nancy (March 2017) Resilient Adaptation Among at-Risk Children: Harnessing Science Toward Maximizing Salutary Environments. *Society for Research in Child Development,* 88(2).

Marcoux, Heather (13 June 2018) Dads Now Spend 3 Times as Much Time with Their Kids than Previous Generations. *Motherly Magazine.*

Matloff, J. (2020) *How to Drag a Body and Other Safety Tips You Hope to Never Need: Survival Tricks for Hacking, Hurricanes and Hazards Life Might Throw at You.* Harper Wave, New York.

May, M. (2018) Cancer with a Human Touched. *Nature*, 556, 7770f.

Morris A.S., Robinson, L., Hays-Grudo, J., Claussen, A., Hartwig, S., and Treat, A. (March 2017) Targeting Parenting in Early Childhood: A Public Health Approach to Improve Outcomes for Children Living in Poverty. *Child Development*, 88(2), 388–397.

Reicher, S.D., and Drury, J. (2020). Don't Personalise, Collectivise. *The Psychologist*. Accessed on 30 March 2020 from https://thepsychologist.bps.org.uk/dont-personalise-collectivise

Steele, Ric, Legerski, John-Paul, Nelson, Timothy, and Phipps, Sean (February 2009) The Anger Expression Scale for Children: Initial Validation among Healthy Children and Children with Cancer. *Journal of Paediatric Psychology*, 34(1), 51–62.

Swanson, Jill, and Berseth, Carol Lynn (July 1987) Continuing Care for the Preterm Infant After Dismissal From the Neonatal Intensive Care Unit. *Mayo Clinic Proceedings*, 62, 613–622.

Weir, Kirsten (September 2017) Maximizing Children's Resilience. *American Psychological Association*, 48(8).

World Health Organization (10 May 2020) *Considerations for School Related Public Health Measures in the Context of COVID 19*. Briefing.

Young Minds Charity Report (March 2020) *Coronavirus: Impact on Young People with Mental Health Needs*. https://youngminds.org.uk/about-us/media-centre/press-releases/coronavirus-having-major-impact-on-young-people-with-mental-health-needs-new-survey

Chapter 8

Barrett, D. (15 April 2020) The Virus Is Giving People; Unusual Vivid Dreams. *National Geographic*.

Blagrove, M., Hale, S., Lockheart, J., Carr, M., Jones, A., and Valli, K. (2019) Testing the Empathy Theory of Dreaming: The Relationships Between Dream Sharing and Trait and State Empathy. *Frontiers in Psychology*, 10, 135.

Hooper, Rowan (9 May 2020) How the Coronavirus Crisis Is Affecting Your Dreams. *New Scientist*, 246(3281), 11.

Jouvet, Michel (1999) *The Paradox of Sleep: The Story of Dreaming*, translated by Laurence Garney. MIT Press, Cambridge, MA.

King's College Survey. https://gbws.cognitron.co.uk/account/consent?next=/ex/task/q_GBIT 2020_demographicsfull

Reicher, S., Drury, J., and Stott, C. (1 April 2020) The Two Psychologies and Coronavirus. *The Psychologist*.

Reicher, S., and Stott, C. (2020) Policing the Coronavirus Outbreak: Processes and Prospects for Collective Disorder. *Policing: A Journal of Policy and Practice*, Briefing April 19.

Smith, N., and Barrett, E. (18 March 2020) Coping with Isolation. *The Psychologist*.

Taquet, M., Quoidbach, J., Gross, J.J., Saunders, K.E.A., and Goodwin, G.M. (2020) Mood Homeostasis, Low Mood, and History of Depression in 2 Large Population Samples. *JAMA Psychiatry*. Published online April 22.

Watson, Galadriel (18 May 2020) Having Coronavirus Nightmares? Here's What You Can Do about Those Bad Dreams. *Washington Post*.

Chapter 9

Ambrose, Jillian (26 April 2020) UK Energy Firms Using Debt Collectors Despite Coronavirus Agreement. *The Guardian*.

BBC News (28 April 2020) *British Airways to Cut up to 12,000 Jobs as Air Travel Collapses*. https://www.bbc.co.uk/news/business-52462660

Carlyle, Thomas (February 1849) Occasional Discourse on the Negro Question. *Fraser's Magazine for Town and Country London*, XL.

Davies, Ellis (4 June 2020) UK New Car Registrations Fell -89% in May, Lowest in the Month Since 1952. *Motor Trader*.

GMjournal.co.uk. (27 April 2020) *Mood homeostasis can help manage depression during Covid-19 lockdown*. https://www.gmjournal.co.uk

International Monetary Fund (14 April 2020) *World Economic Outlook April 2020: The Great Lockdown International Research Department*. https://www.imf.org/en/Publications/WEO/Issues/2020/04/14/World-Economic-Outlook-April-2020-The-Great-Lockdown-49306

Jahoda, Marie (1933) *Marienthal; The Sociography of an Unemployed Community*. Leipzig.

Jouvet, Michel (2000) *The Paradox of Sleep*. MIT Press, Cambridge, MA.

Levine, J.A. (2015) Sick of Sitting. *Diabetologia*, 58(8), 1751–1758.

Lipuma, L. (11 May 2020) COVID 19 Lockdowns Significantly Impacting Global Air Quality. *Advancing Earth and Space Sciences*.

Muenster, Eva, Rueger, Heiko, Ochsmann, Elke, Letzel, Stephan, and Toschke, André M. (2011) Association between Overweight, Obesity and Self-perceived Job Insecurity in German Employees. *BMC Public Health*, 11, 162.

Sharma, Alok (19 April 2020) UK Department for Business, Energy & Industrial Strategy.

Taquet, M., Quoidbach, J., Gross, J.J., Saunders, K.E.A., and Goodwin, G.M. (22 April 2020) Mood Homeostasis, Low Mood, and History of Depression in 2 Large Population Samples. *JAMA Psychiatry*, e200588.

Warr, Peter Bryan (2001) *Psychology in Sheffield: The Early Years*. Sheffield Academic Press, Sheffield.

Chapter 10

Ambrose, Jillian (26 April 2020) UK Energy Firms Using Debt Collectors Despite Coronavirus Agreement. *The Guardian*.

Eurostat European Commission News Release (20 June 2018) *Working from Home in the EU*. https://ec.europa.eu/eurostat/web/products-eurostat-news/-/DDN-20180620-1

International Monetary Fund (2020) *World Economic Outlook, April 2020: The Great Lockdown*. International Monetary Fund, Washington, DC.

Jahoda, Marie, Lazarsfeld, Paul, and Zeisel, Hans (1972) *Marienthal: The Sociography of an Unemployed Community*. Tavistock Publications, London.

Levine, James A. (2015) Sick of Sitting. *Diabetologia*, 58(8), 1751–1758.

Mikes, George (1946) *How to Be an Alien*. Andre Deutsch, London.

NHS Guidelines. https://www.nhs.uk/live-well/healthy-body/how-to-sit-correctly/

Owen, Neville, et al. (2010) Too Much Sitting: The Population Health Science of Sedentary Behavior. *Exercise and Sport Sciences Reviews*, 38(3), 105–113.

Rockette-Wagner, B., Edelstein, S., Venditti, E.M., et al. (2015) The Impact of Lifestyle Intervention on Sedentary Time in Individuals at High Risk of Diabetes. *Diabetologia*, 58(6), 1198–1202.

Warr, Peter Bryan (2001) *Psychology in Sheffield: The Early Years*. Sheffield Academic Press, Sheffield.

Wilmot, E., Edwardson, Charlotte, Achana, Felix, Davies, M., Gorely, Trish, Gray, Laura, Khunti, Kamlesh, Yates, T., and Biddle, Stuart (2011) Sedentary Time in Adults and the Association with Diabetes, Cardiovascular Disease and Death: Systematic Review and Meta-analysis. *Diabetologia*, 55.

Chapter 11

Arias-Reyes, C., and Zubieta-DeUrioste, N. (June 2020) Does the Pathogenesis of SARS-CoV-2 Virus Decrease at High-altitude? *Respiratory Physiology & Neurobiology*, 277, 103443.

Chaddock-Heyman, Laura, Erickson, Kirk, Voss, Michelle, Knecht, Anya, Pontifex, Matthew, Castelli, Darla, Hillman, Charles, and Kramer, Arthur (2013) The Effects of Physical Activity on Functional MRI Activation Associated with Cognitive Control in Children: A Randomized Controlled Intervention. *Frontiers in Human Neuroscience*, 7, 72.

Feuerecker, M., Hauer, Daniela, Toth, Roland, Demetz, F., Hölzl, J., Thiel, Manfred, Kaufmann, Ines, Schelling, G., and Choukèr, A. (2012) Effects of Exercise Stress on the Endocannabinoid System in Humans Under Field Conditions. *European Journal of Applied Physiology*, 112, 2777–2781.

Gliemann, Lasse, Hansen, Camilla Vestergaard, Rytter, Nicolai, and Hellsten, Ylva (August 2019) Regulation of Skeletal Muscle Blood Flow During Exercise. *Current Opinion in Physiology*, 10.

Hallal, P.C., Andersen, L.B., Bull, F.C., et al. (2012) Global Physical Activity Levels: Surveillance Progress, Pitfalls, and Prospects. *The Lancet*, 380(9838), 247–257.

Harber, V.J., and Sutton, J.R. (1984) Endorphins and Exercise. *Sports Medicine*, 1(2), 154–171.

Heyman, E., Gamelin, F., et al. (2012) Intense Exercise Increases Circulating Endocannabinoid and BDNF Levels in Humans: Possible Implications for Reward and Depression. *Psychoneuroendocrinology*, 37, 844–851.

Hughes, John, Waterfield, Angela, Hughes, John, and Kosterlitz, Hans, et al. (1977) Endogenous Opioid Peptides: Multiple Agonists and Receptors. *Nature*, 267, 495–499.

Johnson, Katerina, and Dunbar, Robin (2016) Pain Tolerance Predicts Human Social Network Size. *Nature Scientific Reports*, 6 (25267).

Meyer, Jacob, Crombie, Kevin, Cook, Dane, Hillard, Cecilia, and Koltyn, Kelli. (2019) Serum Endocannabinoid and Mood Changes after Exercise in Major Depressive Disorder. *Medicine & Science in Sports & Exercise*, 51(9), 1909–1917.

Pedisic, Z., Shrestha, N., Kovalchik, S., et al. (2019) Is Running Associated With a Lower Risk of All-cause, Cardiovascular and Cancer Mortality, and Is the More the Better? A Systematic Review and Meta-analysis. *British Journal of Sports Medicine* [published online ahead of print, 4 November 2019]. https://doi.org/10.1136/bjsports-2019-101793

Raichlen, D.A., Foster, A.D., Seillier, A., Giuffrida, A., and Gerdeman, G.L. (2013) Exercise-induced Endocannabinoid Signaling Is Modulated by Intensity. *European Journal of Applied Physiology*, 113(4), 869–875.

Schmidt, M., Egger, F., and Conzelmann, A. (2015) Delayed Positive Effects of an Acute Bout of Coordinative Exercise on Children's Attention. *Perceptual and Motor Skills*, 121(2), 431–446.

Solari, C.D., and Mare, R.D. (2012) Housing Crowding Effects on Children's Wellbeing. *Social Science Research*, 41(2), 464–476.

Sparling, P.B., Giuffrida, A., Piomelli, D., Rosskopf, L., and Dietrich, A. (2003) Exercise Activates the Endocannabinoid System. *Neuroreport*, 14(17), 2209–2211.

Welsh, Jennifer (14 September 2011) Why Laughter May Be the Best Pain Medicine. *The Scientific American*.

Yeung, R.R. (1996) The Acute Effects of Exercise on Mood State. *Journal of Psychosomatic Research*, 40(2), 123–141.

Chapter 12

Asher, Richard (2015) *Talking Sense About Medicine*. Psychology News Press, London.

Benedetti, Fabrizio, Mayberg, Helen S., Wager, Tor D., Stohler, Christian S., and Zubieta, Jon-Kar (November 2005) Neurobiological Mechanisms of the Placebo Effect. *Journal of Neuroscience*, 25(45), 10390–10402.

Collinson, Patrick (8 April 2018) UK Living Rooms Have Shrunk by a Third, Survey Finds. *The Guardian*.

Dunbar, R.I.M., Baron, Rebecca, Frangou, Anna, Pearce, Eiluned, van Leeuwen, Edwin J.C., Stow, Julie, Partridge, Giselle, MacDonald, Ian, Barra, Vincent, and van Vugt, Mark (September 2011) Social Laughter Is Correlated with an Elevated Pain Threshold. *Proceedings of the Royal Society*, 279(1731), 1161–1167.

Hallal, P.C., Andersen, L.B., Bull, F.C., et al. (2012) Global Physical Activity Levels: Surveillance Progress, Pitfalls, and Prospects. *The Lancet*, 380(9838), 247–257. https://doi.org/10.1016/S0140-6736(12)60646-1

Hillard, C.J. (2018) Circulating Endocannabinoids: From Whence Do They Come and Where Are They Going? *Neuropsychopharmacology*, 43(1), 155–172.

Johnson, Katerina, and Dunbar, Robin (April 2016) Pain Tolerance Predicts Human Social Network Size. *Nature Scientific Reports*, 6(25267).

Mandolesi, L., Polverino, A., Montuori, S., et al. (27 April 2018) Effects of Physical Exercise on Cognitive Functioning and Wellbeing: Biological and Psychological Benefits. *Front Psychol*, 9, 509.

Mathers, Colin, Stevens, Gretchen, and Mascarenhas, Maya (2009) *Department of Health Statistics and Informatics in the Information*. Evidence and Research Cluster of the World Health Organization. https://www.who.int/healthinfo/global_burden_disease/GlobalHealthRisks_report_full.pdf

Pedisic, Z., Shrestha, N., Kovalchik, S. et al. (2020) Is Running Associated with a Lower Risk of All-cause, Cardiovascular and Cancer Mortality, and Is the More the Better? A Systematic Review and Meta-analysis. *British Journal of Sports Medicine*, 54(15), 898–905.

Schmidt, Mirko, Egger, Fabienne, and Conzelmann, Achim. (2015). Delayed Positive Effects of an Acute Bout of Coordinative Exercise on Children's Attention. *Perceptual and Motor Skills*, 121(2), 431–446.

Warburton, Darren E.R., et al. (2006) Health Benefits of Physical Activity: The Evidence. *CMAJ: Canadian Medical Association Journal*, 174(6), 801–809.

Chapter 13

Churchill, Winston (1949) *Painting as a Pastime*. Odhams Press Limited, London.

David, Aaronovitch (28 May 2020) When Life's Difficult, Cults Are an Easy Answer Conspiracy Theories and New Age Nonsense Like Universal Medicine Offer Some Middle-class Escapism From Dark Reality. *The Sunday Times*.

Wilmot, Rhi (2 April 2020) Keeping Your Sense of Meaning During Lockdown. *The Psychologist*.

Chapter 14

Andrew, Alison, Cattan, Sarah, Costa Dias, Monica, Farquharson, Christine, Kraftman, Lucy, Krutikova, Sonya, Phimister, Angus, and Sevilla, Alumudena (27 May 2020) *Parents,*

Especially Mothers, Paying Heavy Price for Lockdown. Institute for Fiscal Studies Report. https://www.ifs.org.uk/publications/14861

Bake, B., Larsson, P., Ljungkvist, G., Ljungström, E., and Olin, A-C. (2019) Exhaled Particles and Small Airways. *Respiratory Research*, 20(8). Published online January 11. doi: 10.1186/s12931-019-0970-9

Carothers, Thomas, and Wong, David (4 May 2020) *The Coronavirus Pandemic Is Reshaping Global Protests Carnegie Endowment for International Peace.* https://carnegieendowment.org/2020/05/04/coronavirus-pandemic-is-reshaping-global-protests-pub-81629

Casadevall, Arturo, and Pirofski, Liise-anne (March 2020) The Convalescent Sera Option for Containing COVID-19. *The Journal of Clinical Investigation*, 130(4), 1545–1548.

Duncan, Conrad (May 10, 2020) The Independent. https://www.independent.co.uk/news/world/asia/coronavirus-south-korea-nightclub-spread-second-wave-cases-seoul-a9507596.html
5

Donne, John (1633) *To His Mistress Going to Bed in His Works*, in *Poems 1669* (final 17th century edition). Henry Herringman, London.

Festinger, Leon, Reicken, Henry, and Schacter, Stanley (1956) *When Prophecy Fails.* HarperTorch Books, New York.

Goren, A., Vano, Galvan S., Wambier, C., McCoy, J., et al. (July 2020) A Preliminary Observation: Male Pattern Hair Loss Among Hospitalized COVID-19 Patients in Spain – A Potential Clue to the Role of Androgens in COVID-19 Severity. *Journal of Cosmetic Dermatology*, 19(7), 1545–1547.

Grey Ellis, Emma (2020) The Anti-Quarantine Protests Aren't About COVID-19. *Wired.*

Liu, Sean T.H., Lin, Hung-Mo, Baine, Ian, Wajnberg, Ania, Gumprecht, Jeffrey P., Rahman, Farah, Rodriguez, Denise, Tandon, Pranai, Bassily-Marcus, Adel, Bander, Jeffrey, Sanky, Charles, Dupper, Amy, Zheng, Allen, Altman, Deena R., Chen, Benjamin K., Krammer, Florian, Mendu, Damodara Rao, Firpo-Betancourt, Adolfo, Levin, Matthew A., Bagiella, Emilia, Casadevall, Arturo, Cordon-Cardo, Carlos, Jhang, Jeffrey S., Arinsburg, Suzanne A., Reich, David L., Aberg, Judith A., and Bouvier, Nicole M. (20 May 2020) Convalescent Plasma Treatment of Severe COVID-19: A Matched Control Study. Pre-print. *medRxiv*, 20102236.

Office for National Statistics (7 May 2020) *How Ethnic Groups Vary Across Some of the Social Determinants of Health.*

Resolution Foundation (6 May 2020) *Corona Crisis Could Increase Youth Unemployment by 600,000 This Year – And Scar Young People's Prospects for Far Longer.*

Stapley, Leslie, and Murdock, Nancy (2020) Leisure in Romantic Relationships: An Avenue for Differentiation of Self. *Personal Relationships*, 27(2).

Vogels, Josey (November 2014) *Better Sex in No Time an Illustrated Guide for Busy Couples.* Cleis Press. San Francisco, CA.

Wadman, Meredith (3 June 2020) Why Coronavirus Hits Men Harder: Sex Hormones Offer Clues. *Sciencemag.Org.*

Ward, Alex (20 May 2020) Anti-Lockdown Protests Aren't Just an American Thing. They're a Global Phenomenon. *Vox.*

Warner, Peter (2020) *Young Workers in the Coronavirus Crisis*, in Rutger Bregman (ed.), Humankind. Bloomsbury, London. Resolution Foundation London.

Young Workers in the Coronavirus Crisis (April 2020) *Resolution Foundation.* Findings from the Resolution Foundation's Coronavirus Survey, London.